A-Z MAIDSTONE, CHATHAM GILLINGHA

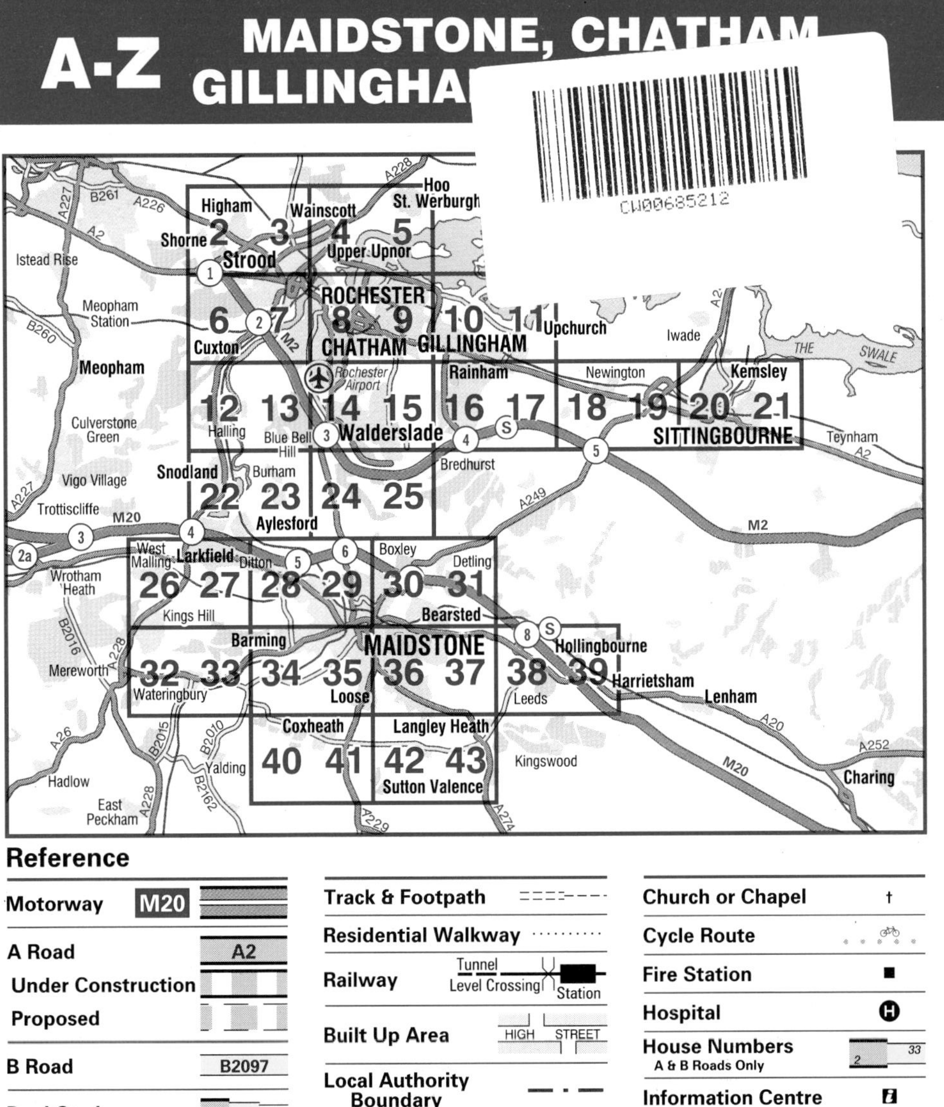

Reference

- Motorway — M20
- A Road — A2
  - Under Construction
  - Proposed
- B Road — B2097
- Dual Carriageway
- One Way Street
  - Traffic flow on A roads is indicated by a heavy line on the drivers' left
- Pedestrianized Road
- Restricted Access
- Track & Footpath
- Residential Walkway
- Railway — Tunnel, Level Crossing, Station
- Built Up Area — HIGH STREET
- Local Authority Boundary
- Posttown Boundary
- Postcode Boundary within Posttown
- Map Continuation — 8
- Car Park selected
- Church or Chapel
- Cycle Route
- Fire Station
- Hospital
- House Numbers A & B Roads Only — 2, 33
- Information Centre
- National Grid Reference — 160
- Police Station
- Post Office
- Toilet
  - with facilities for the Disabled

Scale 1:19,000

3⅓ inches to 1 mile or 5.26 cm to 1 km

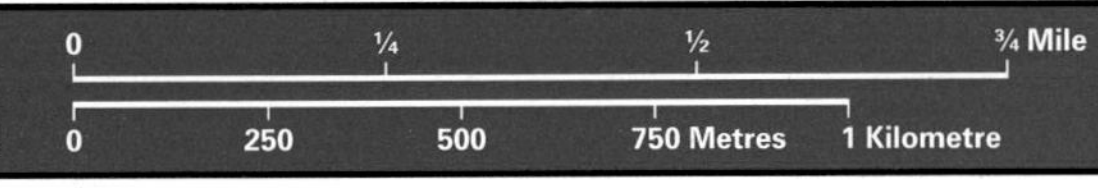

Copyright of Geographers' A-Z Map Company Limited

Head Office : Fairfield Road, Borough Green, Sevenoaks, Kent TN15 8PP Tel: 01732 781000
Showrooms : 44 Gray's Inn Road, London WC1X 8HX Tel: 020 7440 9500

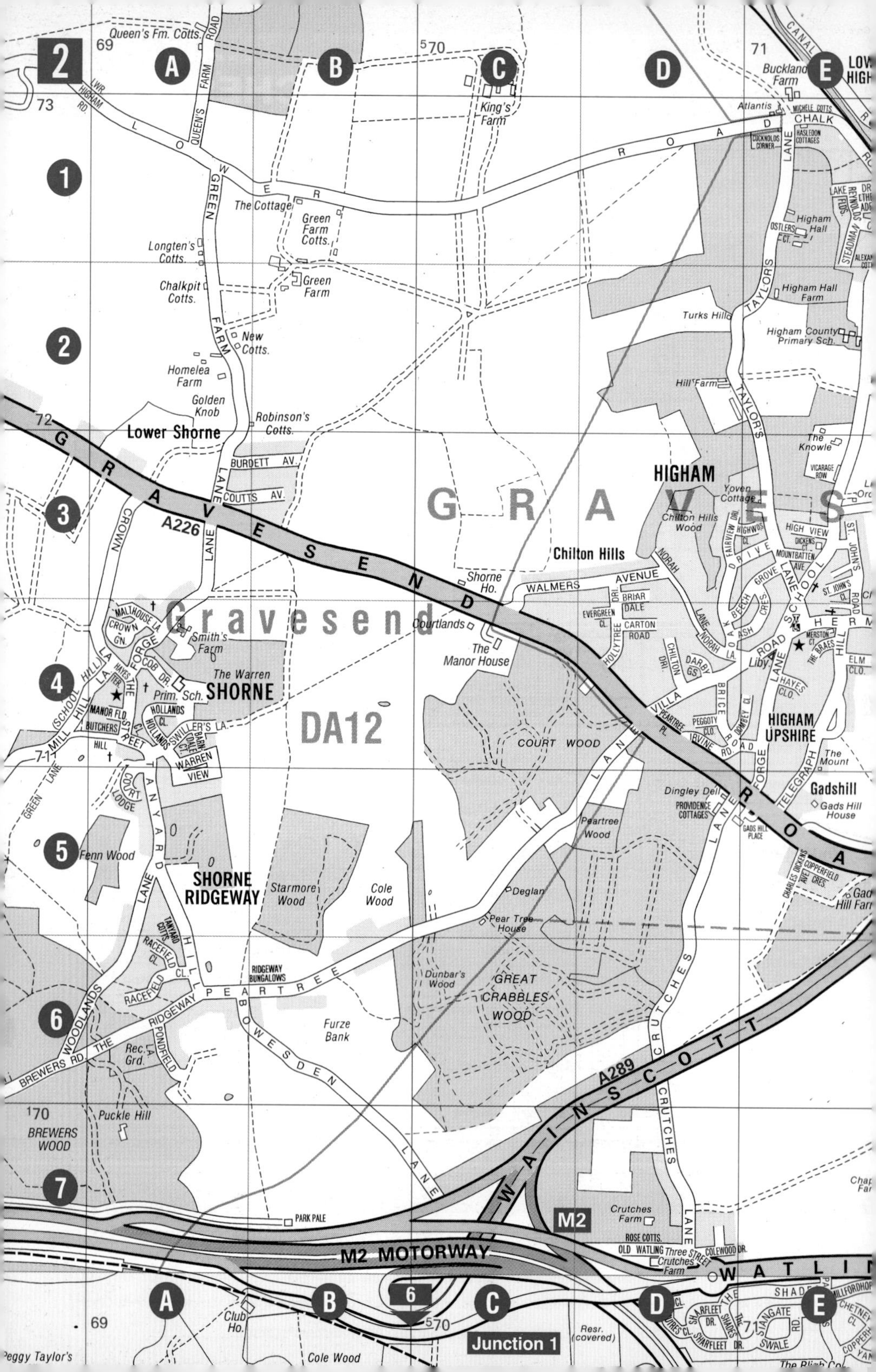

2
Queen's Fm. Cotts.
Lower Shorne
GRAVESEND ROAD
A226
Gravesend
SHORNE
DA12
SHORNE RIDGEWAY
HIGHAM
Chilton Hills
HIGHAM UPSHIRE
Gadshill
COURT WOOD
GREAT CRABBLES WOOD
Starmore Wood
Cole Wood
Fenn Wood
Furze Bank
Puckle Hill
BREWERS WOOD
Peartree Wood
Dunbar's Wood
WAINSCOTT
A289
M2 MOTORWAY
M2
Junction 1
Crutches Farm
Three Street Crutches Farm
Club Ho.
Resr. (covered)
PARK PALE
LOWER ROAD
King's Farm
Green Farm
Green Farm Cotts.
The Cottage
Longten's Cotts.
Chalkpit Cotts.
New Cotts.
Homelea Farm
Golden Knob
Robinson's Cotts.
Buckland Farm
Atlantis
Higham Hall
Higham Hall Farm
Turks Hill
Higham County Primary Sch.
Hill Farm
The Knowle
Yoven Cottage
Chilton Hills Wood
Shorne Ho.
Courtlands
The Manor House
Smith's Farm
The Warren
Prim. Sch.
Dingley Dell
PROVIDENCE COTTAGES
GADS HILL PLACE
Gads Hill House
The Mount
Deglan
Pear Tree House
RIDGEWAY BUNGALOWS
Rec. Grd.
ROSE COTTS.
OLD WATLING
COLEWOOD DR.
Cole Wood
Peggy Taylor's

3
Gore Green
Higham
Lillechurch
Lee Green
Mockbeggar
Rochester
MEDWAY
ME3
ME2
STROOD
Strood
Wood Bungalow
Reservoir
Cricket Ground
Cherry Garden Cottages
Two Gates Farm
Dusty Hill
White House Farm
Lee Green Cottages
Lee Green Cotts.
Little Lodge Cott.
Cliffe Lodge
Dairy Cottages
Schoolhouse Cottages
Rose Cottages
Higham Mill
Hillyfield
Chalkpit Cottage
Stonehorse Cottages
Stone House Farm
Nursery
Brickhouse Farm
The Cottage
Gouge Farm
Sole Street Farm
Amie Lodge
Holly Tree Cottage
Bunters Farm
Hollywood House
Dillywood Cottages
Little Hermitage
West Lodge
Fieldgate Cottages
Brompton Farm
Temple School
Swimming Pool
Broom Hill
Abbey Ct. Sch.
Chapter Farm Cottages
Pavilion
Tennis Cts
Sports Grnd.
Gordon Co. Inf. & Jun. Sch.
Hilltop C.P. Sch.
Playing Field
Prim. Sch.
Comm. Cen.
Priory
Recn. Grnd.
Swim. Pool
Synthetic Pitch
Strood Sports Cen.
Westfield Business Centre
The Bungalow Home Rest
Gore Green Farm
B2000
A289
A226
B2108
A2
NORTHERN BY PASS
GRAVESEND ROAD
LOWER ROCHESTER ROAD
ROCHESTER ROAD
TWOGATES HILL
BUNTERS HILL
COMMON ROAD
LONDON ROAD
FRINDSBURY RD.
STATION RD.
FARM ROAD
HOLLYWOOD LA.
4
7

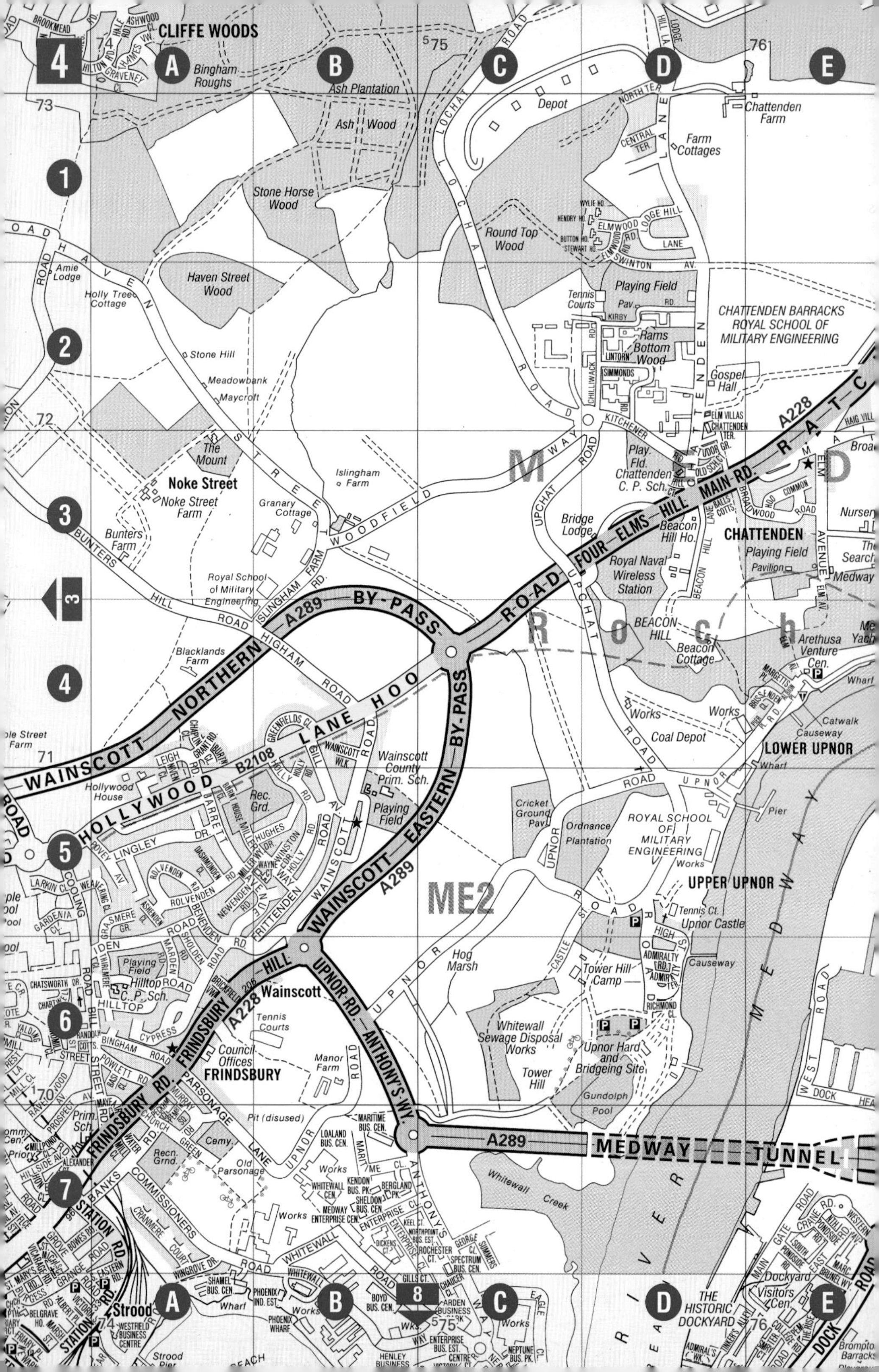

4
CLIFFE WOODS
Bingham Roughs
Ash Plantation
Ash Wood
Stone Horse Wood
Haven Street Wood
Round Top Wood
Depot
Chattenden Farm
Farm Cottages
CENTRAL TER.
NORTH TER.
LODGE HILL
ELMWOOD RD.
SWINTON AV.
Playing Field
Tennis Courts
Rams Bottom Wood
CHATTENDEN BARRACKS ROYAL SCHOOL OF MILITARY ENGINEERING
Gospel Hall
LOCHAT ROAD
KITCHENER
Amie Lodge
Holly Tree Cottage
Stone Hill
Meadowbank
Maycroft
The Mount
Noke Street
Noke Street Farm
Bunters Farm
Granary Cottage
Islingham Farm
WOODFIELD WAY
Royal School of Military Engineering
Blacklands Farm
BUNTERS HILL ROAD
HIGHAM ROAD
A289 BY-PASS
FOUR ELMS HILL MAIN RD.
A228
Bridge Lodge
Royal Naval Wireless Station
BEACON HILL
Beacon Cottage
Play. Fld.
Chattenden C. P. Sch.
CHATTENDEN
Playing Field
Pavilion
Arethusa Venture Cen.
Works
Coal Depot
LOWER UPNOR
Wharf
Catwalk
Causeway
Pier
WAINSCOTT NORTHERN
LANE HOO
B2108
HOLLYWOOD
Hollywood House
Rec. Grd.
Wainscott County Prim. Sch.
Playing Field
EASTERN BY-PASS
WAINSCOTT
A289
ME2
Cricket Ground Pav.
Ordnance Plantation
ROYAL SCHOOL OF MILITARY ENGINEERING
Works
UPPER UPNOR
Tennis Ct.
Upnor Castle
UPNOR ROAD
Hog Marsh
Tower Hill Camp
Causeway
Whitewall Sewage Disposal Works
Upnor Hard and Bridgeing Site
Tower Hill
Gundolph Pool
RIVER MEDWAY
A228
Wainscott
Tennis Courts
Council Offices
FRINDSBURY
Manor Farm
Playing Field
Hilltop C. P. Sch.
FRINDSBURY RD.
UPNOR RD.
ANTHONY'S WY.
Pit (disused)
Cemy.
Recn. Grnd.
Old Parsonage
A289
MEDWAY TUNNEL
Whitewall Creek
Works
STATION RD.
Strood
Wharf
THE HISTORIC DOCKYARD
Dockyard Visitors Cen.
3
8
A B C D E
1 2 3 4 5 6 7

DEANGATE RIDGE GOLF COURSE
Playing Field
Sports Ground
Club
Mill Farm
MILL FARM COTTAGES
Riversview
Rayes Lodge
FRANCES COTTS.
Tile Barn
STURDEE COTTS.
Abbots Ct. Lodge
Sch.
White Ho. Farm
STREET FARM COTTS.
Street Farm
Surgery
Sundown
Stonebridge
Rosehill
Coronation Bungalow
HOO ST. WERBURGH
Hoo St. Werburgh C. P. Sch.
The Hundred of Hoo Comp. Sch.
The Hundred of Hoo Nursery Sch.
Village Hall Rec. Grd.
Abbots Court Cottages
STOKE RD. BUS. CEN.
NURSERY GDNS.
Broad Street
Hoo Swimming Pool
Liby.
The Elms Medical Cen.
WILLOW GRANGE
Playing Field
Lib.
Church Farm
Sewage Works
Hoo Lodge Cottage
Cockham Farm
COCKHAM COTTAGES
ME3
Hoo Lodge
Old Plantation
THE COPSE
HOO MARINA PARK
Cockham Wood
Saxon Shore Way
Gull Down Plantation
Works
Hoo Marina
Breakwater
Ford Marsh
West Hoo Creek
HOO SALT MARSH
Finsborough Ness Slipway
RIVER MEDWAY
Mud
St. Mary's Island
Playing Field
Chatham Maritime
ME4
Medway (Chatham) Docks
Bull Nose
East Wharf
Gillingham Piers
Pontoon
GILLINGHAM REACH
A228
A289
GILLINGHAM—NORTHERN—LINK—ROAD
ME7
Uni. of Greenwich
Gillingham Marina
Causeway
Strand Leisure Centre
Boating Pool
Gasholder Station
Putting Green
GILLINGHAM MARSHES
PIER RD.
9
77
78
79
73
72
71
70

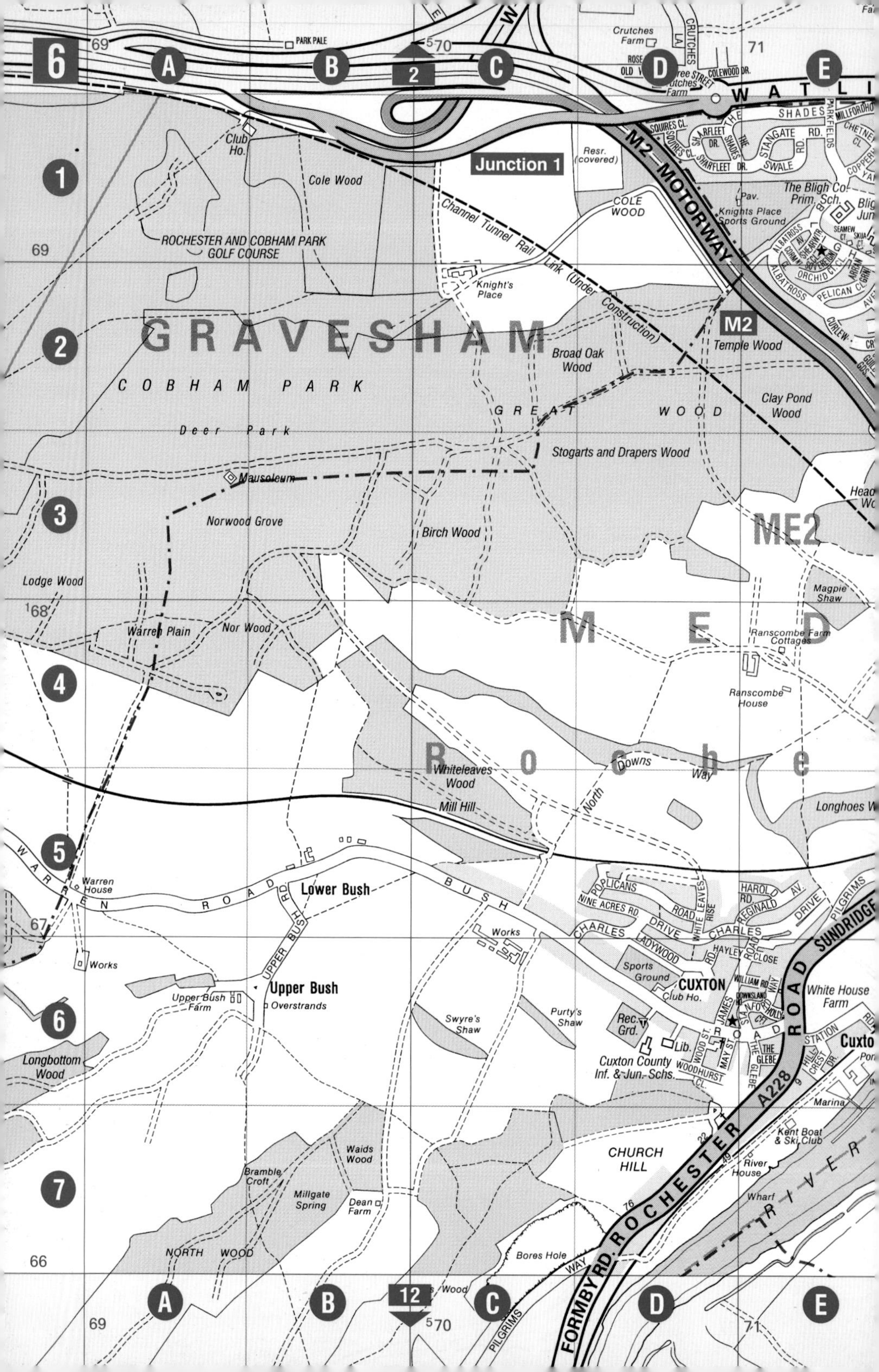

A
B
C
D
E
1
2
3
4
5
6
7
2
12
PARK PALE
Crutches Farm
CRUTCHES LA.
COLEWOOD DR.
WATLI
Junction 1
Resr. (covered)
M2 MOTORWAY
SQUIRES CL.
SHARFLEET DR.
THE SHADES
STANGATE RD.
SWALE
PARKFIELDS
MILLFORD
The Bligh Co. Prim. Sch.
Knights Place Sports Ground
Pav.
ALBATROSS AV.
ORCHID CT.
PELICAN CL.
CURLEW
Club Ho.
Cole Wood
COLE WOOD
ROCHESTER AND COBHAM PARK GOLF COURSE
Channel Tunnel Rail Link (Under Construction)
Knight's Place
GRAVESHAM
COBHAM PARK
Broad Oak Wood
Temple Wood
M2
Clay Pond Wood
GREAT WOOD
Deer Park
Stogarts and Drapers Wood
Mausoleum
Norwood Grove
Birch Wood
ME2
Lodge Wood
Magpie Shaw
MED
Warren Plain
Nor Wood
Ranscombe Farm Cottages
Ranscombe House
Whiteleaves Wood
North Downs Way
Mill Hill
Longhoes W
WARREN ROAD
Warren House
Lower Bush
BUSH
UPPER BUSH RD.
POPLICANS
NINE ACRES RD
ROAD
WHITE LEAVES RISE
HAROLD RD.
REGINALD AV.
DRIVE
PILGRIMS
SUNDRIDGE
CHARLES DRIVE
LADYWOOD
HAYLEY CLOSE
Works
Sports Ground
CUXTON
Club Ho.
Works
Upper Bush
Upper Bush Farm
Overstrands
White House Farm
Swyre's Shaw
Purty's Shaw
Rec. Grd.
Lib.
JAMES
WOOD ST.
MAY ST.
THE GLEBE
STATION
HILL CREST DR.
ROAD
A228
Cuxton County Inf. & Jun. Schs.
WOODHURST CL.
Longbottom Wood
Marina
Kent Boat & Ski Club
CHURCH HILL
ROCHESTER
River House
Wharf
RIVER
Waids Wood
Bramble Croft
Millgate Spring
Dean Farm
NORTH WOOD
Bores Hole
PILGRIMS WAY
FORMBY RD.
69
70
71
68
67
66

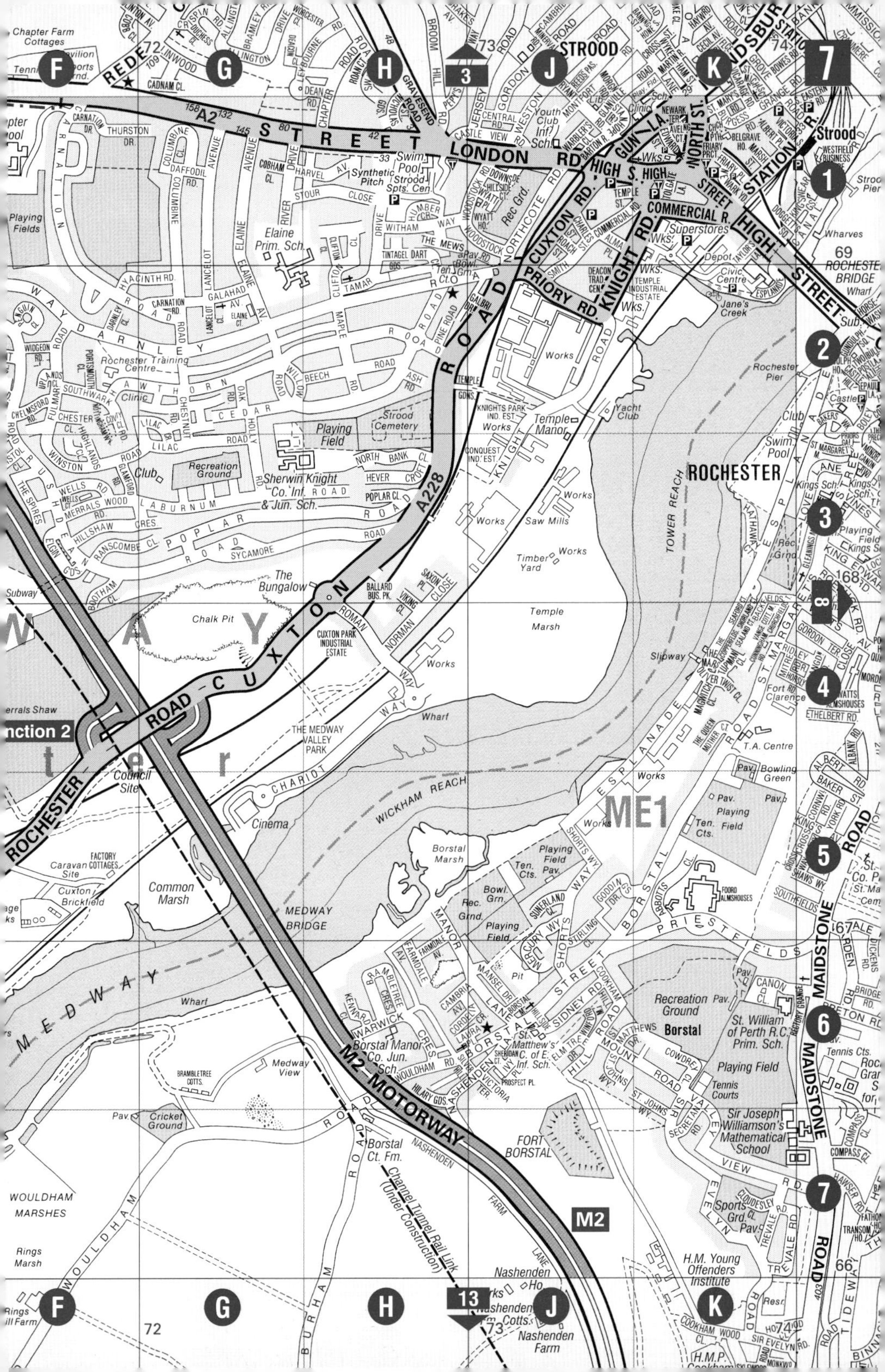

7
3
13
8
F
G
H
J
K
1
2
3
4
5
6
7
STROOD
ROCHESTER
ME1
LONDON RD.
STREET
A2
A228
CUXTON ROAD
ROCHESTER ROAD
M2 MOTORWAY
M2
HIGH STREET
STATION RD.
NORTH ST.
COMMERCIAL RD.
KNIGHT RD.
PRIORY RD.
GRAVESEND ROAD
MAIDSTONE ROAD
BORSTAL STREET
BORSTAL ROAD
ESPLANADE
ST. MARGARET'S ST.
PRIESTFIELDS
VALLEY VIEW RD.
WOULDHAM ROAD
BURHAM ROAD
NASHENDEN FARM LANE
MEDWAY
MEDWAY BRIDGE
WICKHAM REACH
TOWER REACH
Temple Marsh
Borstal Marsh
Common Marsh
WOULDHAM MARSHES
Rings Marsh
Strood
Superstores
Civic Centre
Rochester Pier
Jane's Creek
Temple Manor
Yacht Club
Temple Industrial Estate
Knights Park Ind. Est.
Conquest Ind. Est.
Cuxton Park Industrial Estate
Ballard Bus. Pk.
The Medway Valley Park
Chalk Pit
The Bungalow
Cinema
Council Site
Caravan Site
Factory Cottages
Cuxton Brickfield
Elaine Prim. Sch.
Rochester Training Centre
Strood Cemetery
Playing Field
Recreation Ground
Sherwin Knight Co. Inf. & Jun. Sch.
Strood Spts. Cen.
Synthetic Pitch
Swim. Pool
Youth Club
Fort Clarence
Watts Almshouses
T.A. Centre
Bowling Green
Foord Almshouses
St. William of Perth R.C. Prim. Sch.
Sir Joseph Williamson's Mathematical School
Borstal Manor Co. Jun. Sch.
St. Matthew's C. of E. Inf. Sch.
Fort Borstal
H.M. Young Offenders Institute
Borstal Ct. Fm.
Channel Tunnel Rail Link (Under Construction)
Nashenden Farm
Nashenden Cotts.
Cricket Ground
Medway View
Bramble Tree Cotts.
Sports Grd.
Rochester Bridge
Wharves
Wharf
Works
Saw Mills
Timber Yard
Chapter Farm Cottages
Playing Fields
Junction 2
Subway

A
B
C
D
E
1
2
3
4
5
6
7
4
7
14
ME2
ME1
ME4
Strood
Rochester
ROCHESTER
Chatham
CHATHA
BROMPTON
THE HISTORIC DOCKYARD
Dockyard Visitors Cen.
Brompton Barracks
FRINDSBURY PENINSULA
MEDWAY CITY ESTATE
RIVER MEDWAY
CHATHAM REACH
LIME HOUSE REACH
BRIDGE REACH
GASHOUSE POINT
ROCHESTER BRIDGE
Strood Pier
Rochester Pier
Limehouse Wharf
Blue Boar Pier
Medway Heritage Centre
Kitchener Barracks
Fort Amherst
Riverside Gardens
Sun Pier
Ship Pier
Radio Kent
Town Hall Gds.
Magistrates Ct.
Pentagon Centre
Central Hall Theatre
Troy Town
BARTHOLOMEW'S HOSPITAL
Kent Institute of Art & Design
Fort Pitt Grammar Sch. for Girls
Mid Kent Coll. of Higher & Further Ed.
Victoria Gds.
St. John Fisher Catholic Comp. Sch.
St. Michael's R.C. Prim. Sch.
Balfour Co. Jun. Sch.
Chatham Mental Hlth. Cen.
Rochester Grammar Sch. for Girls
Sir Joseph Williamson's Mathematical School
Delce Co. Inf. & Jun. Schs.
Wisdom Hospice
Glencoe Co. Inf. & Jun. Schs.
Redvers Cen.
Chatham Gram. Sch. for Boys & Chatham Sth. Sch.
The Thomas Aveling Sch.
Warren Wood Co. Prim. Sch.
St. Peter's Co. Prim. Sch.
St. Margaret's Cemetery
Rochester Hlth. Cen.
Recreation Ground
Football Ground
CORPORATION ST.
HIGH STREET
NEW RD.
NEW A2 RD.
CITY WAY
A229
A230
A231
A2310
DOCK ROAD
MAIDSTONE ROAD
STAR HILL
THE BROOK
HIGH ST.
BOAR LANE
ROCHESTER AVENUE
CASTLE AVENUE
WOOD ST.
NEW STREET
RAILWAY ST.
ROYAL EAGLE CL.
NEPTUNE WAY
SIR THOMAS LONGLEY RD.
WHITEWALL ROAD
COMMISSIONERS ROAD

9
GILLINGHAM
ME7
ME5
Gillingham Piers
Pontoon
Causeway
Gillingham Marina
Strand Leisure Centre
Boating Pool
Gasholder Station
The Strand
Putting Green
Tennis Cts.
GILLINGHAM MARSHES
Wharf
PIER ROAD
A289
GADS HILL
DANES HILL
MEDWAY RD.
B2004
PRINCE ARTHUR RD.
GILLINGHAM NORTHERN LINK ROAD
Royal School of Military Engineering
Royal Engineers Mus.
Lower Lines
Prince Arthur Pk.
Indoor Bowl. Cen.
Black Lion Field
Black Lion Leisure Cen.
BROMPTON RD.
A231
Cricket Ground
Sports Ground
Great Lines
Cemetery
Hillyfields County Jun. Sch.
St. Mary's R.C. Prim. Sch.
Railway Street Ind. Est.
Gillingham
Depot
Bowling Grn.
Balmoral Gds.
Gillingham F.C.
JEFFERY ST.
CANTERBURY ST.
DUNCAN RD.
NELSON ROAD
Bus Sta.
Upbury Manor High Sch.
Playing Field
MEDWAY HOSPITAL
Napier County Prim. Sch.
Council Offices
Gillingham Park
Municipal Bldgs.
Nursing Home
Byron Prim. Sch.
The Robert Napier School
Playing Fields
The Gillingham Coll. & Woodlands Cty. Prim. Sch.
Woodlands Cen.
Day Care Centres
Rec. Ground
Play ground
GILLINGHAM GOLF COURSE
Club Ho.
Langton Playing Fields
GILLINGHAM NORTHERN LINK ROAD
CHATHAM HILL
A2
RAINHAM ROAD
WATLING ST.
SOVEREIGN BOULEVARD
UPPER LUTON ROAD
B2156
LUTON ROAD
Chatham Grammar Sch. for Girls
Beacon Hill
Works
Resrs. (Cov.)
Sports Ground
Drill Hall
Star Farm
Darland Banks
Warehouses
GILLINGHAM BUSINESS CENTRE
LUTON
Daisy Banks
Golf Driving Range
Water Works
Luton Rec. Ground
Hale Farm
CAPSTONE RD.
NORTH DANE WAY

10
RIVER MEDWAY
A
B
C
D
E
79
580
81
Nor Marsh
Gillingham Creek
COPPERHOUSE MARSHES
Ferol Peak
GILLINGHAM MARSHES
CINQUE PORT MARSHES
STEELFIELD IND. EST.
Wharf
Foundry
Works
Sports Ground
Saxon Shore Way
GADS HILL
DANES HILL
GILLINGHAM NORTHERN LINK ROAD
LOWER RAINHAM ROAD
Equestrian Centre
Walnut Tree Farm
EASTCOURT MEADOWS
Horrid Hill
Grange
Grange Farm
Mill Hill
Mill Hill Farm
B2004
RIVERSIDE COUNTRY PARK
Sharp's Green
Visitor's Centre
Grench Manor
Whetstead
East Court Farm
ME7
Lower Twydall
Greenbank Farm
Mariners Farm
WOODLANDS ROAD
HAZLEMERE DRIVE
A289
Ladds Corner
168
9
Cemetery
Sports Ground
Little London Farm
Manor Farm
Little York Farm
York Farm
CORNWALLIS AVENUE
Gillingham Coll. & Woodlands Cty. Prim. Sch.
Woodlands Cen.
Day Care Centres
BREDGAR ROAD
BEECHINGS INDUSTRIAL CENTRE
Engineering Works
BEECHINGS WAY
EASTCOURT LANE
Rec. Grnd.
Comty. Centre
Recreation Ground
Lower Rainham
Pump Farm
GILLINGHAM GOLF COURSE
Featherby Inf. & Jun. Schools
BROADWAY
Clinic
Lib.
TWYDALL
TWYDALL LANE
PUMP LANE
MEDWAY
67
ELMFIELD
Langton Playing Fields
Dane Court Sch.
Vinall Park
Twydall Inf. & Jun. Schs.
R.C. Prim. Sch.
Thames View County Inf. Sch.
Rainham Mark Gram. Sch.
Thames View County Jun. Sch.
Gillingham
WATLING STREET A2
Club
Factory
Sports Ground
Warehouses
GILLINGHAM BUSINESS PARK
Ice Bowl
Works
Training Cen.
Reservoir
Playing Fields
Splashes Waterpark
Cozenton Park
LONDON ROAD
A2
A278
HOATH WAY
GILLINGHAM BUSINESS CENTRE
66
16
Warehouses
The Howard School
Rainham Sch.
St. Margaret's C.of E. Jun. & County Inf. Sch.

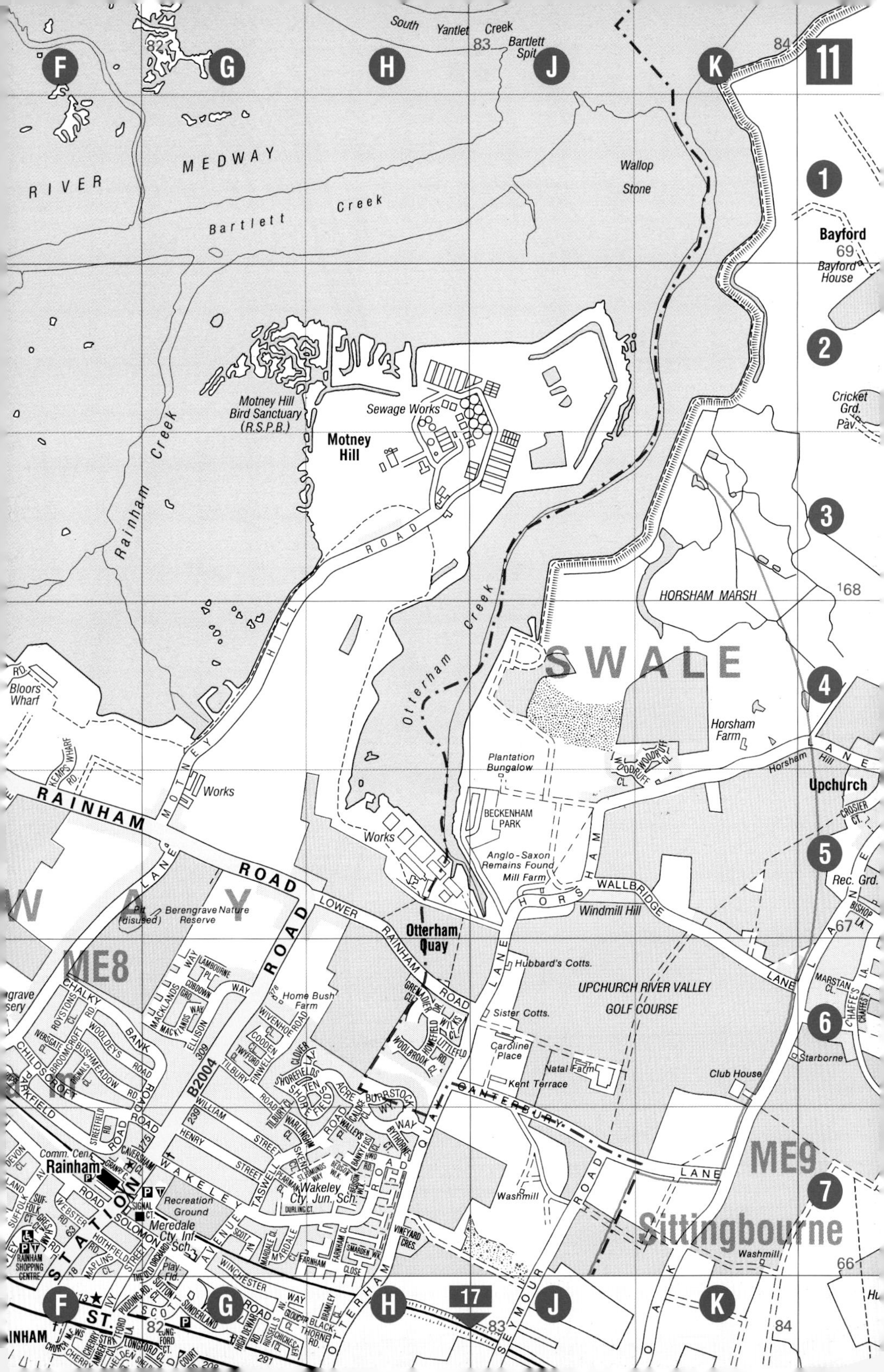

11
South Yantlet Creek
Bartlett Spit
RIVER MEDWAY
Bartlett Creek
Wallop Stone
Bayford
Bayford House
Cricket Grd. Pav.
Motney Hill Bird Sanctuary (R.S.P.B.)
Sewage Works
Motney Hill
Rainham Creek
MOTNEY HILL ROAD
Otterham Creek
HORSHAM MARSH
SWALE
Horsham Farm
Plantation Bungalow
WOODRUFF CL.
Horsham Hill Lane
Upchurch
CROSIER CT.
Bloors Wharf
KEMPS WHARF RD.
RAINHAM ROAD
Works
BECKENHAM PARK
Anglo-Saxon Remains Found
Mill Farm
Rec. Grd.
WALLBRIDGE LANE
Windmill Hill
HORSHAM LANE
BISHOP LA.
MOTNEY LANE
Pit (disused)
Berengrave Nature Reserve
LOWER RAINHAM ROAD
Otterham Quay
ME8
Hubbard's Cotts.
UPCHURCH RIVER VALLEY GOLF COURSE
MARSTAN CL.
CHAFFES LA.
Home Bush Farm
Sister Cotts.
Caroline Place
Natal Farm
Kent Terrace
Starborne
Club House
CANTERBURY LANE
ME9
Sittingbourne
Washmill
SEYMOUR ROAD
OAK LANE
CHALKY BANK ROAD
WOOLDEYS ROAD
BUSHMEADOW RD.
CHILDSCROFT ROAD
PARKFIELD
B2004
WILLIAM STREET
HENRY STREET
WAKELEY ROAD
TASWELL
Wakeley Cty. Jun. Sch.
Comm. Cen.
Rainham
STATION ROAD
Recreation Ground
Meredale Cty. Inf. Sch.
Play. Fld.
SOLOMON RD.
WINCHESTER WAY
OTTERHAM QUAY LANE
VINEYARD CRES.
RAINHAM SHOPPING CENTRE
HIGH ST.
SUNDERLAND
SCOTT AV.
17
82
83
84
66
67
68
69
168
291
F
G
H
J
K
1
2
3
4
5
6
7

NORTH WOOD
May's Wood
Bores Hole
Millgate Spring
Dean Farm
Home Bavins
Thistly Spring Wood
White Pit (Disused)
Stonyfield Shaw
Stonyfield House
Scrub Wood
The Warren
Wingate Wood
North Halling
ROCHESTER ROAD
FORMBY ROAD
A228
HALLING BY-PASS
SNODLAND BY-PASS
ME2
PILGRIMS WAY
Works
Chalk Pit
Lake
Upper Halling Court
VICARAGE ROAD
North Pit (Disused)
Bottom Pit (Disused)
Nut Hole Pit (Dis.)
South Pit (Disused)
DEAN HILL
MEDWAY
Upper Halling
CHAPEL LA.
THE BROWNDENS RD.
MEADOW CRES.
BARN MEADOW
MONARCH HILL
RESERVOIR COTTS.
HALLING
New Town
Caravan Park
Sewage Works
Halling
Manor Farm
Marsh Lodge Farm
Halling Fresh Marsh
Halling Salt Marsh
Halling Common
RIVER MEDWAY
Wharf
Rochester
WOULDHAM
Haymans Wharf
Wouldham Marshes
Starkey Farm
The Cottage
Halling County Prim. Sch.
Dock (Disused)
Pond
Whitting's Farm
The Homestead
Home Farm
Home Farm Cottages
The Cedars
LADDS LANE
Snodland
ME6
Holborough
Tennis Cts.
Sports Ground
Bowling Green
Holborough Quarry
WHITE DYKE
Holborough Marshes
PETERS WORKS
OLD CHURCH ROAD
HIGH STREET
Holborough Mews
Ponds

6
22

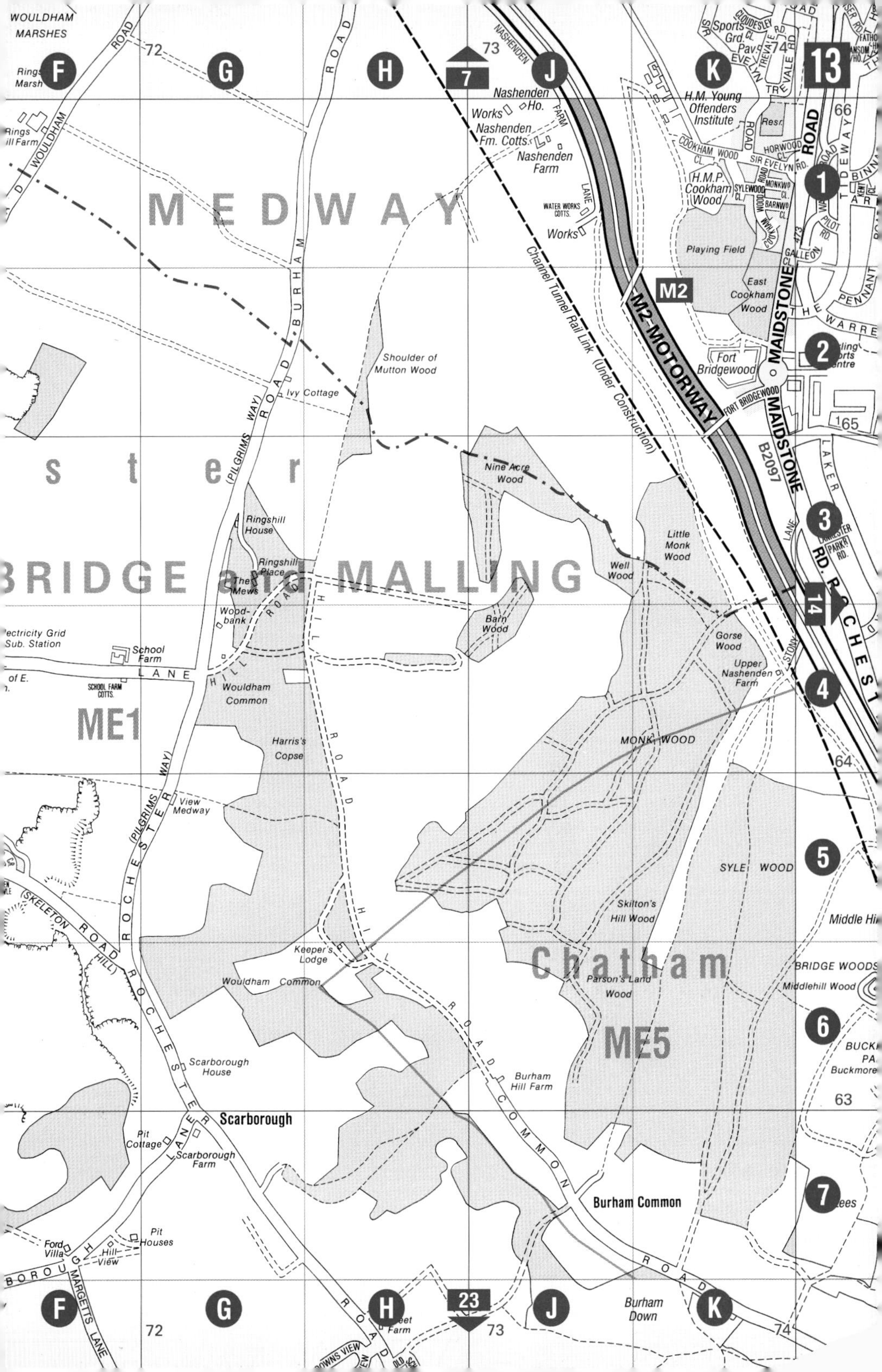

13
MEDWAY
BRIDGE and MALLING
Chatham
ME1
ME5
WOULDHAM MARSHES
Rings Marsh
Ringshill Farm
WOULDHAM ROAD
Nashenden Ho.
Works
Nashenden Fm. Cotts.
Nashenden Farm
NASHENDEN FARM LANE
WATER WORKS COTTS.
H.M. Young Offenders Institute
Sports Grd.
Pav.
H.M.P. Cookham Wood
Playing Field
East Cookham Wood
Fort Bridgewood
M2
M2 MOTORWAY
MAIDSTONE ROAD
B2097
Channel Tunnel Rail Link (Under Construction)
Shoulder of Mutton Wood
Ivy Cottage
BURHAM ROAD (PILGRIMS WAY)
Nine Acre Wood
Little Monk Wood
Well Wood
Barn Wood
Gorse Wood
Upper Nashenden Farm
Ringshill House
Ringshill Place
The Mews
Wood-bank
HILL ROAD
Electricity Grid Sub. Station
School Farm
SCHOOL FARM COTTS.
LANE
Wouldham Common
Harris's Copse
MONK WOOD
SYLE WOOD
Skilton's Hill Wood
Parson's Land Wood
View Medway
ROCHESTER ROAD (PILGRIMS WAY)
(SKELETON HILL) ROAD
Keeper's Lodge
Wouldham Common
Middle Hill
BRIDGE WOODS
Middlehill Wood
Scarborough House
Burham Hill Farm
Scarborough
Pit Cottage
Scarborough Farm
Burham Common
COMMON ROAD
Pit Houses
Ford Villa
Hill View
MARGETTS LANE
Burham Down
F
G
H
J
K
72
73
74
64
63
65
66
7
14
23
1
2
3
4
5
6
7

14
A
B
C
D
E
8
13
24
1
2
3
4
5
6
7
74
75
76
66
165
64
63
MAIDSTONE ROAD B2097
CITY WAY A229
MAIDSTONE ROAD A230
HORSTED WY.
MAIDSTONE ROAD A229
M2 MOTORWAY
M2
ROCHESTER ROAD B2097
WALDERSLADE WOODS A2045
MAIDSTONE RD. BY-PASS A229
BLUE BELL HILL
Junc. 3
ME1
ME4
ME5
Rochester
Chatham
TONBRIDGE and MALLING
Playing Field
Rec. Grd.
The Thomas Aveling Sch.
Warren Wood Co. Prim. Sch.
Chatham Gram. Sch. for Boys & Chatham Sth. Sch.
Coney Banks
Playing Fields
Bishop's Hoath Wood
Miniature Golf Course
Snodhurst Bottom
Snodhurst Wood
Wayfield Co. Prim. Sch.
Fort Horsted
Park & Ride (Sat. only)
Mid Kent College
Mid Kent College of Higher & Further Education
Horsted Farm
Playing Field
Stirling Sports Centre
Sports Fld.
Tennis Courts
Works
East Cookham Wood
Fort Bridgewood
ROCHESTER AIRPORT
Superstore
HORSTED RETAIL PARK
Superstores
Hotel
Caravan Pk.
Scout Hut
Bradfields School
Ridge Meadow County Prim. Sch.
Hook Meadow
Greenacre & Walderslade Girls Schs.
Weeds Wood
Oaklands Jun. & Infs. Schools
St. Thomas More R.C. Prim. Sch.
Walderslade C. P. Sch.
Rec. Grnd.
WALDERSLADE
Walderslade Bottom
Taddington Wood
Tunbury County Prim. Sch.
Tunbury Wood
Gravel Hill
Coal Bottom
Gorse Wood
Upper Nashenden Farm
Channel Tunnel Rail Link (Under Construction)
SYLE WOOD
Middle Hill
Go-kart Track
BRIDGE WOODS
Middlehill Wood
Swimming Pool
BUCKMORE PARK
Buckmore Wood
Sports Hall
Shall Hook Wood
Lord Lees
Sports Ground
Cemetery
BOURNVILLE AV.
LETCHWORTH
CHATHAM GROVE
WALDERSLADE RD.
MAGPIE HALL
THE RIDGEWAY
ROOSEVELT AVENUE
WAYFIELD RD.
CHURCHILL AV.
ARETHUSA ROAD
THE WARREN
WILSON AVENUE
SNODHURST AVENUE
HURSTWOOD
GEORGE AVENUE
WATSON AV.
CHESTNUT AV.
TUNBURY AVENUE
ROBIN HOOD LANE
LOWER WALDERSLADE
SUSSEX DRIVE
ROAD
FOSTINGTON WAY
HOOD RD.
LAURIE GRAY

15
9
16
25
F
G
H
J
K
1
2
3
4
5
6
7
77
78
79
Daisy Banks
Golf Driving Range
Water Works
Luton
Kingsdale Court
Depot
Hale
Hale Farm
Playing Field
EAST HILL
Darland
Visitors Centre
Capstone Farm Country Park
Kingfisher County Primary School
GROVE WOOD
Whitewall Farm
Alpine Ski Centre
Chestnut Plantation
Drowhill Woods
Hempstead
Princes Park
Gillingham
ME7
North Dane Wood
Sharsted Cottages
Sharsted Farm
South Wood
HOOK WOOD
Little Knox
Moorcroft
The Woodlands
Lidsing Copse
Great Knocks
Holt Wood
Ballen's Rough
Leisure Centre
Gibraltar Farm
Gibraltar Cottages
ELM COURT INDUSTRIAL ESTATE
Smallholding
Chapel Garden
Lordswood Co. Jun. & Prim. Schs.
St. Benedicts R.C. Prim. Sch.
Lords Wood
MAIDSTONE
Comm. Cen.
Health Cen.
Swingate Co. Inf. Sch.
Spinners Acre Co. Jun. Sch.
Roots Wood
Sindal's Shaw
Reeds
Seeburg
Lidsing Court Farm
Gillingham Business Centre
Warehouses
NORTH DANE WAY
B2156
CAPSTONE ROAD
SHARSTED WAY
HEMPSTEAD ROAD
LIDSING ROAD
KINGSWAY
WALDERSLADE WOODS
ALBEMARLE ROAD
BALLENS ROAD
LORDSWOOD LANE
BOXLEY ROAD
PRINCES AVENUE
CHAPEL LANE
FORGE LANE
HAM LANE
PEAR TREE LANE
DARLAND AVENUE
STAIR ROAD
HAMELIN ROAD
HALE

16
A
B
C
D
E
1
2
3
4
5
6
7
10
15
79
5 80
81
66
65
64
63
Warehouses
CENTURION
BAILEY DR.
VALENTINE
SARACEN CL.
SCIMITAR CL.
Works
GRANT CL.
CHIEFTAIN CL.
Training Cen.
GUARDIAN CT.
Works
Reservoir
VANCOUVER DR.
CHARLOTTE DRIVE
JEFFERSON
LONDON
RD.
AVENUE
Lib.
Playing Fields
The Howard School
CALEDONIAN CT.
THAMES
ROBERTS
HARVEY RD.
CENTURY
NURSERY ROAD
SALISBURY
St. Margaret's C.of E. Jun. & County Inf. Sch.
BROADVIEW
HERBERT
ARTHUR
ORCHARD
HAMELIN RD.
BAILEY
AMBLEY GREEN
DRIVE
AMBLEY
CAMPUS
CRUSADER CL.
THE COURTYARD
Ambley Wood
GOODS VEHICLE TEST CENTRE
West Hoath Wood
STAR
HOATH WAY
A278
SYLVAN RD.
EDWIN ROAD
Warehouses
Factory
COURTENEY ROAD
Factory
Sports Ground
Rainham Sch. for Girls
CRABTREE RD.
OLDFIELD CL.
DERWENT WAY
STRATFORD AV.
HATHAWAY CT.
BENDON WAY
CHERITON
HIGHFIELD RD.
THE GOLDINGS
PLATTERS FARM LODGE
PLATTERS
Platters Park
MARSHALL ROAD
LYNDHURST
Bryony Sch.
BROCKENHURST
LANCASTER CT.
CAMELLIA CL.
AVENUE
MAIDSTONE ROAD
VERNERS
BEACON CL.
ELMSTONE
BETTESCOMBE
NORREYS RD.
Playing Field
ROAD
SANDOWN DR.
WINDERMERE DR.
KENILWORTH GDNS.
WENTWORTH DR.
Spekes Bottom
GROVE WOOD
East Hoath Wood
HOATH LANE
M E D W A Y
DURHAM ROAD
KENILWORTH
CAMBRIDGE RD.
ASQUITH RD.
SPRINGVALE
THE WHEELERS
SWAIN RD.
CHALFONT DR.
TANKER HILL
SUNNINGDALE DR.
GAINSBOROUGH CL.
BARLEYCORN
PLOUGHMANS WAY
HARVESTERS
PEAR TREE LANE
HARROW
THE EVERGLADES
Chestnut Plantation
Playing Field
Pav.
GLENWOOD
HINTON CL.
CRES.
HEMPSTEAD ROAD
SPEKES ROAD
GRASSY GLADE
WOODSIDE
DEANWOOD DR.
NAPWOOD CL.
WOODPECKER GLADE
CHESHAM DRIVE
MOSSY GLADE
GREENFINCHES
WATERS PL.
PIPPIN CROFT
LOMBARDY CL.
HICKORY DELL
COPPERGATE
DRIVE
PINE
GROVE
LEAFY GLADE
FELLOWS CL.
CHAMBERLAIN CT.
THE HAZELS
BREDHURST
LAKEWOOD DR.
LINEACRE
CAMPLESHON RD.
IDENWOOD
HALLWOOD
Fox Burrow Wood
Parkwood County Inf. & Jun. Schs.
DUKES
SHEPHERDS GATE
EVERGREEN CL.
GILBERT CL.
CEDAR GROVE
Hempstead
HEMPSTEAD
FAIRVIEW
WIGMORE ROAD
Rec. Grnd.
EDWARDS CL.
CARVORAN WAY
ST. MARGARETS DR.
DREWERY DR.
Comm. Cen.
Fair View County Prim. & Jun. Schs.
DONET CL.
LEEANDOWN
PARK WOOD GREEN SHOPPING CEN.
Comm. Cen.
Health Cen.
Park Wood
WYVILL CL.
PARKER CL.
GOODALL
BARLOW CL.
DOLPHIN
MARYLAND CT.
HONEY
LAMPLIGHTERS
COBBLESTONES
PADDOCKS
Lib.
Hempstead County Jun. Sch.
FERNDOWN
NORMAN CL.
MAGNOLIA AV.
PRIMROSE AV.
FOULDS CL.
AVE.
Liby
South Wood
HONEYSUCKLE CL.
CLOSE
BIRCH
MEDLAR GRO.
KINGSDOWN CL.
MEADOWDOWN CL.
WILDWOOD GLADE
WIGMORE
Playing Fields
THANET RD.
READSCROFT
CAPEL CL.
LOVELACE
BEKE RD.
CHUTE CL.
CULPEPPER
HARDINGE CL.
CHIPSTEAD
MOYLE CL.
LYALL WY.
FERRIER CL.
TYLER DRIVE
BAYS
ALMOND
MAGDALEN CL.
LAVENDA
THISTLEDOWN CL.
MULBERRY CL.
TAMARIND CL.
Whitegate Wood
GEORGIAN WAY
HANOVER DR.
PRINYS DR.
PEVEREL GREEN
NARES
HAWBECK RD.
Little Knox
BARNCROFT DR.
THE OLD CARRIAGE WAY
CHAPEL
ME7
MELODY CL.
GRAIN RD.
RUTLAND PL.
Dean Wood Co. Prim. Schs.
PLOMLEY CL.
CLAVELL CL.
HUNSTANTON CL.
MIERSCOURT
Ryetop Wood
The Woodlands
Lidsing Copse
CLERMONT
DRIVE
HEMPSTEAD VALLEY SHOPPING CENTRE
Subway
BLOWERS WOOD GRO.
HOUGHTON AVE.
LAMBSFRITH
HARTY AV.
LIME CT.
Reservoir
RYCAUT CL.
School
Community Centre
BURNHAM WK.
Smallholdings
SHARSTED WAY
MARTIN RISE
LULLINGSTONE
ROAD
FOWLER CL.
CHART PL.
SEDLEY CL.
WOLLASTON CL.
WALSINGHAM
Brooms Wood
Chapel Garden
THE LANDOR CT.
SANDY DELL
HADLEIGH CT.
MARQUIS DR.
COPPER BEECH
Blowers Wood
REGENCY CL.
DEANWOOD DRIVE
Brooms Wood
Beeches Brooms Wood
LIDSING ROAD
CHAPEL LANE
MAIDSTONE RD.
Junction 4
M2
M2-MOTORWAY
Duddingstone
HILL
Arosea
Long Lane Wood
Woodsview
MATTS HILL
MAIDSTONE
Abbotts Ct. Farm
STREET
KEMSLEY
ROAD
WHITE HILL RD.
Greatlenn Wood
FORGE
Seeburg
BREDHURST
Woodlea
Paris Farm
Kemsley Street Farm
Court Lodge
Kemsley Street
Purple Hill
Stone Acre Wood
LIDSING RD.
LANE
Lidsing Court Farm
Bredhurst C.of E. Prim. Sch.
STREET

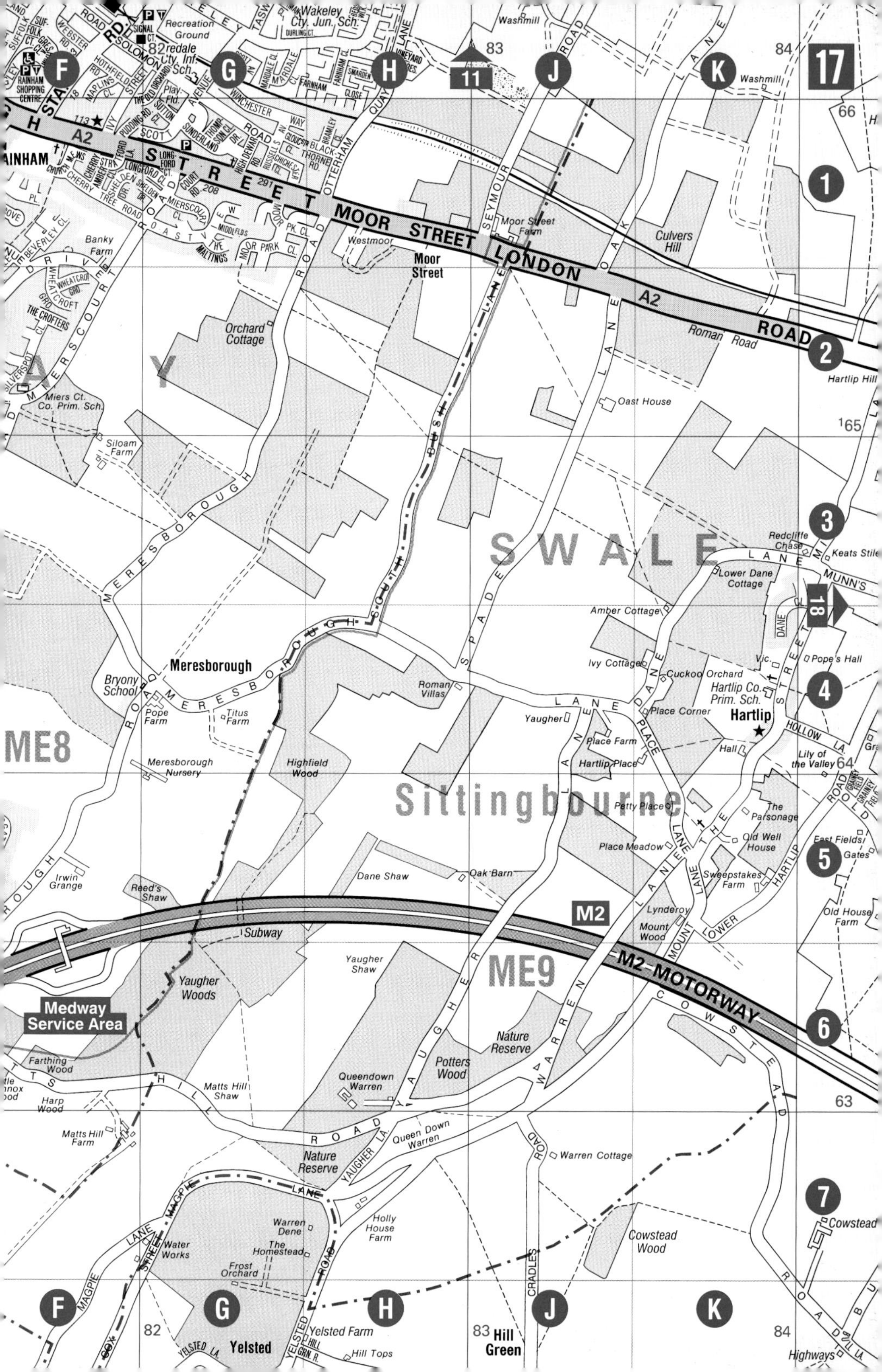
17
Recreation Ground
Wakeley Cty. Jun. Sch.
Washmill
Rainham Shopping Centre
Solomon Rd.
Signal Ct.
Hothfield Rd.
Naplins Cl.
Play. Fld.
Pudding Rd.
Sutton Cl.
Scott Avenue
Winchester Way
Sunderland Dr.
High Dewar Rd.
Russells Av.
Gloucester Rd.
Chichester Cl.
Thorne Rd.
Bramley Cl.
Blackthorne Rd.
Farnham Cl.
Smarden Close
Vineyard Lane
Quay Lane
Otterham Quay Lane
Rainham
A2
High Street
Moor Street
London Road
Roman Road
Church Ms.
Cherry Amber Cl.
Stratford La.
Longford Ct.
Longford Cl.
Cherry Tree Road
Mierscourt Cl.
Mierscourt Road
Oast View
The Maltings
Moor Park Cl.
Westmoor
Moor Street Farm
Seymour Road
Beverley Cl.
Banky Farm
Wheatcroft Gro.
The Crofters
Silverspot Cl.
Mierscourt Road
Drive
Culvers Hill
Orchard Cottage
Oak Lane
Oast House
Hartlip Hill
Miers Ct. Co. Prim. Sch.
Siloam Farm
Meresborough Road
Bush Lane
Spade Lane
SWALE
Redcliffe Chase
Keats Stile
Lower Dane Cottage
Munn's Lane
Amber Cottage
Dane Cl.
Ivy Cottage
Cuckoo Orchard
Vic.
Pope's Hall
Hartlip Co. Prim. Sch.
Hartlip
Place Corner
Street
Hollow La.
Meresborough
Bryony School
Roman Villas
Yaugher
Place Farm
Hartlip Place
Pope Farm
Titus Farm
Hall
Lily of the Valley
Dane Lane
Place Lane
ME8
Meresborough Nursery
Highfield Wood
Sittingbourne
Petty Place
The Parsonage
Old Well House
East Fields
Gates
Place Meadow
Irwin Grange
Reed's Shaw
Dane Shaw
Oak Barn
Sweepstakes Farm
Hartlip Road
Lower Mount Lane
Old House Farm
Lynderoy
Mount Wood
M2
Subway
M2 Motorway
Cowstead Road
Medway Service Area
Yaugher Woods
Yaugher Shaw
ME9
Yaugher Lane
Warren Lane
Nature Reserve
Potters Wood
Farthing Wood
Harp Wood
Matts Hill Shaw
Matts Hill Road
Queendown Warren
Matts Hill Farm
Queen Down Warren
Cradles Road
Warren Cottage
Magpie Lane
Warren Dene
Holly House Farm
Cowstead
Cowstead Wood
Water Works
The Homestead
Frost Orchard
Street
Cox Street
Yelsted Road
Yelsted La.
Yelsted
Yelsted Farm
Hill Grn. R.
Hill Tops
Hill Green
Highways
F
G
H
J
K
1
2
3
4
5
6
7
11
18
82
83
84
63
64
65
66

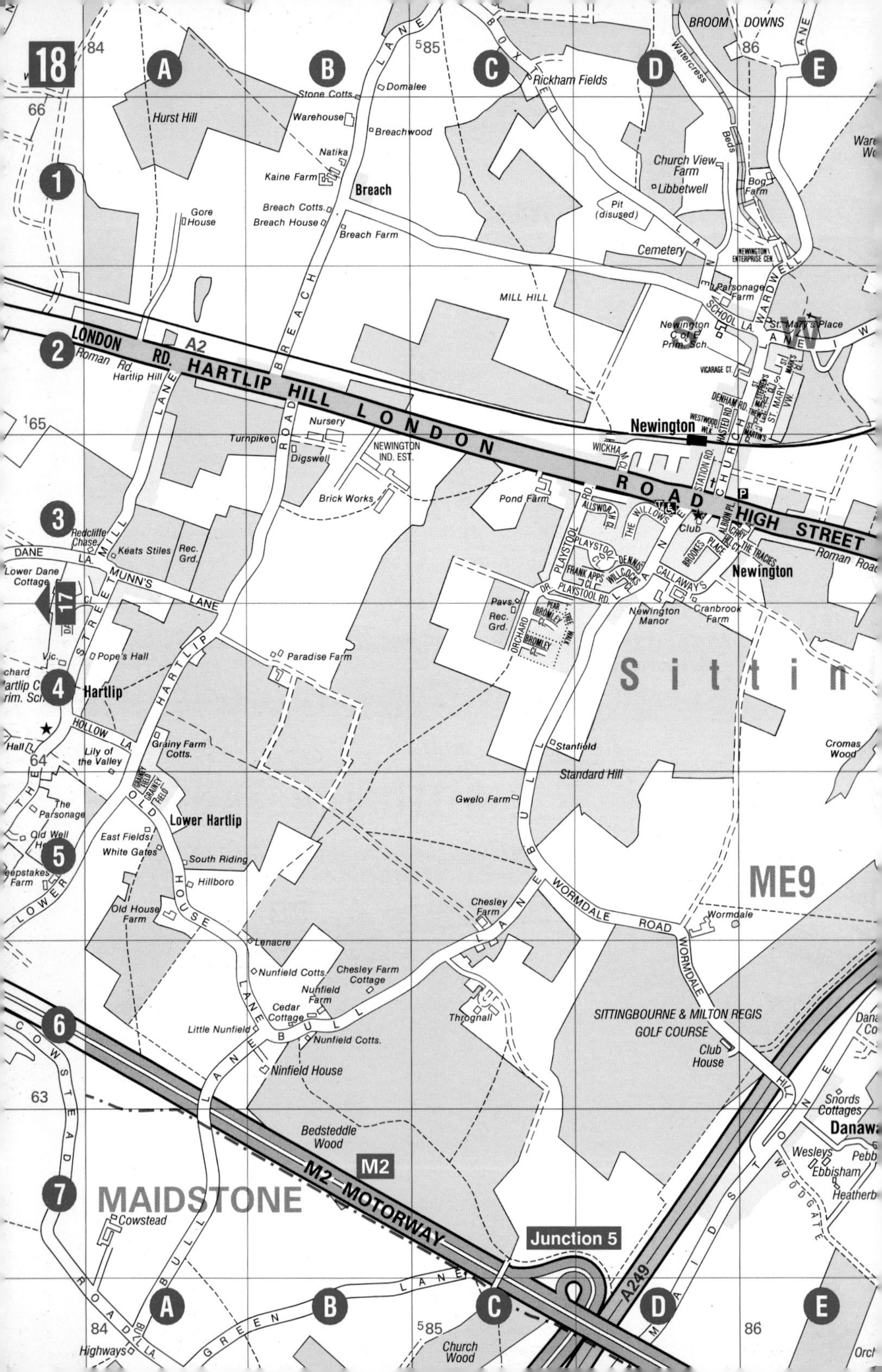

Hurst Hill
Stone Cotts
Domalee
Warehouse
Breachwood
Natika
Kaine Farm
Breach
Gore House
Breach Cotts.
Breach House
Breach Farm
Rickham Fields
BROOM DOWNS
Watercress Beds
Church View Farm
Libbetwell
Pit (disused)
Bog Farm
Cemetery
NEWINGTON ENTERPRISE CEN.
Parsonage Farm
MILL HILL
Newington C of E Prim. Sch.
St. Mary's Place
SCHOOL LA.
WARDWELL LANE
LONDON RD.
A2
Roman Rd.
Hartlip Hill
HARTLIP HILL LONDON
LONDON ROAD
Nursery
Turnpike
Digswell
NEWINGTON IND. EST.
Brick Works
Newington
Pond Farm
HIGH STREET
Roman Road
Club
Newington
Newington Manor
Cranbrook Farm
CALLAWAYS
PLAYSTOOL RD.
Pavs.
Rec. Grd.
Redcliffe Chase
Keats Stiles
Rec. Grd.
DANE LA.
Lower Dane Cottage
MUNN'S LANE
17
Pope's Hall
Paradise Farm
Hartlip
HOLLOW LA.
Lily of the Valley
Grainy Farm Cotts.
Sittin
Stanfield
Standard Hill
Cromas Wood
Gwelo Farm
Lower Hartlip
The Parsonage
Old Well
East Fields
White Gates
South Riding
Hillboro
Old House Farm
Chesley Farm
WORMDALE ROAD
Wormdale
ME9
Lenacre
Nunfield Cotts.
Chesley Farm Cottage
Nunfield Farm
Cedar Cottage
Little Nunfield
Nunfield Cotts.
Ninfield House
Thrognall
SITTINGBOURNE & MILTON REGIS GOLF COURSE
Club House
Snords Cottages
Bedsteddle Wood
M2
M2 MOTORWAY
MAIDSTONE
Cowstead
COWSTEAD ROAD
Junction 5
A249
Wesleys
Ebbisham
GREEN LANE
BULL LANE
Highways
Church Wood
84
585
86
66
165
64
63
A
B
C
D
E
1
2
3
4
5
6
7

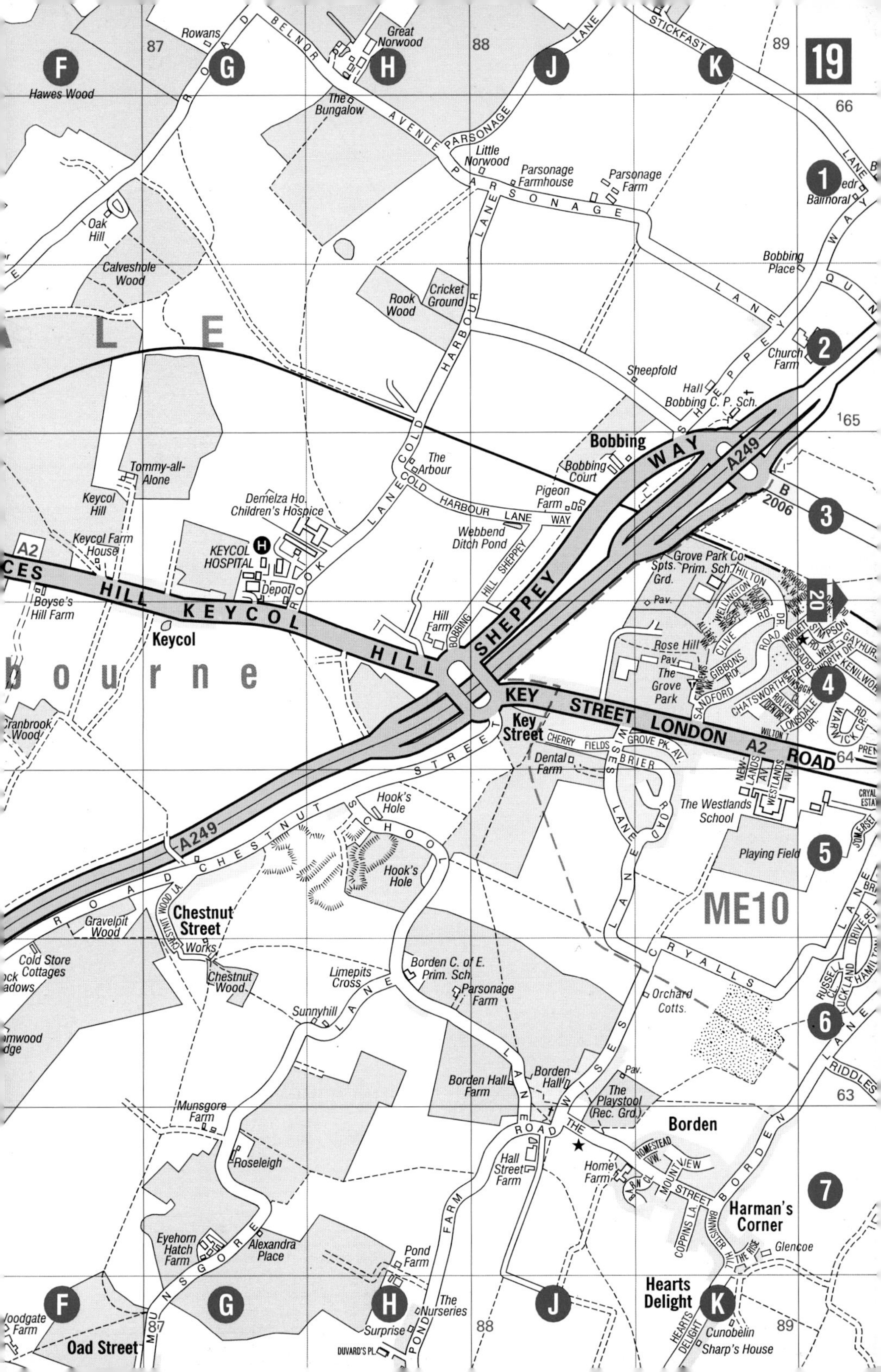
Rowans
Great Norwood
Hawes Wood
The Bungalow
BELNOR AVENUE
PARSONAGE LANE
STICKFAST LANE
Little Norwood
Parsonage Farmhouse
Parsonage Farm
Balmoral
Oak Hill
Calveshole Wood
Bobbing Place
Rook Wood
Cricket Ground
HARBOUR LANE
COLD HARBOUR LANE
SHEPPEY WAY
QUINTON
Church Farm
Sheepfold
Hall
Bobbing C. P. Sch.
Bobbing
Bobbing Court
The Arbour
Tommy-all-Alone
Keycol Hill
Demelza Ho. Children's Hospice
Pigeon Farm
Webbend Ditch Pond
B 2006
A249
A2
Keycol Farm House
KEYCOL HOSPITAL
Depot
Grove Park Co. Prim. Sch.
Spts. Grd.
Pav.
Boyse's Hill Farm
KEYCOL HILL
Keycol
Hill Farm
BOBBING HILL
SHEPPEY
HILTON
WELLINGTON
CLIVE
Rose Hill
The Grove Park
GIBBONS RD.
SANDFORD
CHATSWORTH
LONSDALE DR.
WARWICK CR.
KENILWORTH
GAYHURST
SIMPSON
WOOLLETT RD.
Cranbrook Wood
KEY STREET
Key Street
LONDON ROAD A2
CHERRY FIELDS
GROVE PK. AV.
BRIER ROAD
Dental Farm
NEWLANDS AV.
WESTLANDS AV.
The Westlands School
CRYALLS
Hook's Hole
SCHOOL LANE
CHESTNUT STREET
ROAD
Playing Field
Gravelpit Wood
Chestnut Street
CHESTNUT WOOD LA.
Works
ME10
Cold Store Cottages
Chestnut Wood
Limepits Cross
Borden C. of E. Prim. Sch.
Parsonage Farm
Orchard Cotts.
RUSSELL CL.
BUCKLAND
HAMILTON
DRIVE
Sunnyhill
Borden Hall Farm
Borden Hall
The Playstool (Rec. Grd.)
Borden
WISES LANE
RIDDLES
Munsgore Farm
THE ROAD
HOMESTEAD VW.
MOUNT VIEW
Roseleigh
Hall Street Farm
Home Farm
MOUNT STREET
BORDEN LANE
Harman's Corner
COPPINS LA.
BANNISTER HILL
THE RISE
Glencoe
Eyehorn Hatch Farm
Alexandra Place
Pond Farm
FARM
MUNSGORE
Hearts Delight
HEARTS DELIGHT
The Nurseries
Surprise
POND
DUVARD'S PL.
Cunobelin
Sharp's House
Woodgate Farm
Oad Street
Swale
Sittingbourne
F G H J K
87 88 89
66 65 64 63
1 2 3 4 5 6 7
20

20
89
A
Howt Green
B
590
Depot
BRAMBLEFIELD LA.
C
GROVEHURST
Kemsley
D
KEMSLEY
E
91
COLDHARBOUR LANE
RIDHAM AV.
Church Marshes Country P
66
STICKFAST LANE
Stickfast Farm
Nether Toes
1
Blossoms
Llanbedr
Balmoral
ME9
A249
Blue Houses
Playing Fld.
B2005
BEAUVOIR DRIVE
NEWMAN
ATTLEE WAY
Bobbing Place
SHEPPEY
QUINTON
Church Farm
2
Quinton Farm House
Regis Manor C.P. Sch.
Court Regis
Sch.
SAFFRON WY.
ROAD
Depot
Playing Field
P. Sch.
65
KNIGHTSFIELD RD.
THE MEADS AV.
VICARAGE ROAD
NORTH
CRESCENT
LANGLEY
Sittingbourne & Kemsley Light Railway
Sewage Works
3
B2006
MILTON REGIS
Rec. Grd.
TRINITY TRADING ESTATE
Prim. Sch.
Mus.
Works
Depots
Roman Burial Ground
ME10
MILL WAY
19
Middle Junction
Western Junction
Factory
Chalkwell
St. PAUL'S ST.
Depot
Gas
Wks.
EUROLINK COMMERCIAL
4
Sittingbourne
SITTINGBOURNE INDUSTRIAL PARK
Crown Quay
Dolphin Sailing Barge Mus.
BOURNCRETE HOUSE
Paper Mill
Mill
Depot
Works
Hall
LONDON A2
ROAD
EUROLINK B2006 WY.
EUROLINK
64
CRYALLS ESTATE
WESTLANDS
Playing Field
5
Depot
Homewood Co. Inf. Sch.
Play. Fld.
Barrow Gro. Co. Prim. Sch.
Swale Cen.
WEST ST.
HIGH
ST. MICHAEL'S
Sittingbourne
A2 ROAD
STREET
EAST STREET
THE BELL SHOP. CEN
Leisure Cen.
Lib.
T.H.
MIDDLETON CT.
HOMEWOOD
6
AVENUE OF REMEMBERANCE
Play. Fld.
Borden Gram. Sch.
Club
Pav.
Rec. Ground
Cemy.
Rec. Grd.
Sch.
South Av. Inf. & Jun. Schs.
College
Pav.
63
SITTINGBOURNE
SITTINGBOURNE MEMORIAL HOSP.
Spicer Homes
Highsted Sch. for Girls & Fulston Manor Sch.
Play. Fld.
St Peter's R.C. Prim. Sch.
Minterne Co. Inf. & Jun. Schs.
Sch.
Sports Ground
Pav.
Cemy.
ME9
MINTERNE
7
Harman's Corner
Glencoe
Fulston Manor
Chilton Manor Farm
A
B
C
D
E
89
590
King George's Field
91

Kemsley Town
Castle Rough
Kemsley Marshes
Sittingbourne and Kemsley Light Railway
Milton Creek
Saxon Shore Way
Little Murston
Works
Shipbreakers
Church Wharf
Tonge Corner Farm
Woods Cottages
Tonge Corner
Tonge Corner Cottages
Cheke's Court
Wilford Court
Blacketts Road
Telegraph Hill
East Hall Wood
Church (remains of)
Gas Rd.
Anchor Business Pk.
Brickmakers Ind. Est.
D2 Trading Estate
Central Park Sittingbourne F. C.
Mere Ct.
Church Rd. Bus. Cen.
Castleacres Ind. Pk.
Castle Rd. Tech. Cen.
Drywall Ind. Est.
Castle Rd. Bus. Precinct
Club
Rec. Grd.
Hugh Price Cl.
ME9
The Oast Golf Cen.
West Tonge Farm
East Hall
Oak Rd.
Dolphin Rd.
Dolphin Pk.
Cremers Rd.
Sunny Bank
Gorse Rd.
Murston Co. Jun. Sch.
Hall
Inf. Sch.
Ceres Ct.
Churchill Ho.
Portland Av.
Eagles Cl.
Wells Ho.
East Hall La.
St. Giles Houses
Murston
Tonge Road
Lomas Road
Swan Cl.
Home View Cl.
Smeed Cl.
Keham Rd.
All Saints Rd.
Gordon Cl.
Rosebery Cl.
Bunces Farm
Wheatcroft Cl.
Harkness Ct.
Grove
Drive
Peel Drive
Salisbury Cl.
Lansdown Drive
Palmerston Wk.
Gladstone Dr.
Beaconsfield Rd.
Keswick Av.
Vincent Rd.
Ambleside
Coombe
Birch Ho.
Woodberry
Willow Ho.
Elm Gr.
Thomas Rd.
Cowper Rd.
Harold Rd.
Murston Rd.
Tonge Castle (site of)
Tonge Mill
Scraps Hill Cottages
Cistern Cottages
Lower Road
Mill Pond
Scraps Hill
Lane
Stones Farm
Lansdowne Co. Prim. Sch.
Play. Fld.
Tonge
Hempstead Farm
Canterbury Road
Common-Wealth Close
Canterbury Rd.
Green Ways
Prince Charles Av.
Middle Way
Rectory Rd.
Rectory Play. Field
Nutfields
St. John's Av.
Cambridge Rd.
Snipeshill
Fox Hill
The Street
Bapchild
St. Thomas a Becket's Spring
Hempstead Lane
Ashmead
Cricket Ground
Pav.
London Road
A2
Sports Centre
Avenue
Sittingbourne Comm. Coll & The St. Thomas Sch.
Prim. Sch.
School Lane
Ashtead Dr.
Morris Court Cl.
Doubleday Drive
Lords Cl.
Whitred
Bapchild Court
Hempstead House
Seedmeal Cottages
Radfield
Little Radfield
Temple Gdns.
Cedar Cl.
Glebe
Wanstree
Step Style
Penn Cl.
Blenheim Rd.
Ridge
Fairlea
Warren Cl.
Playing Field
Muddy Lane
St. Lawrence Cl.
Lane
Panteny Lane
The Old Vicarage
Morris Court
Haywood
Church Street
Tully
Little Dully
Sittingbourne
F
G
H
J
K
1
2
3
4
5
6
7
92
93
94
63
64
65
66

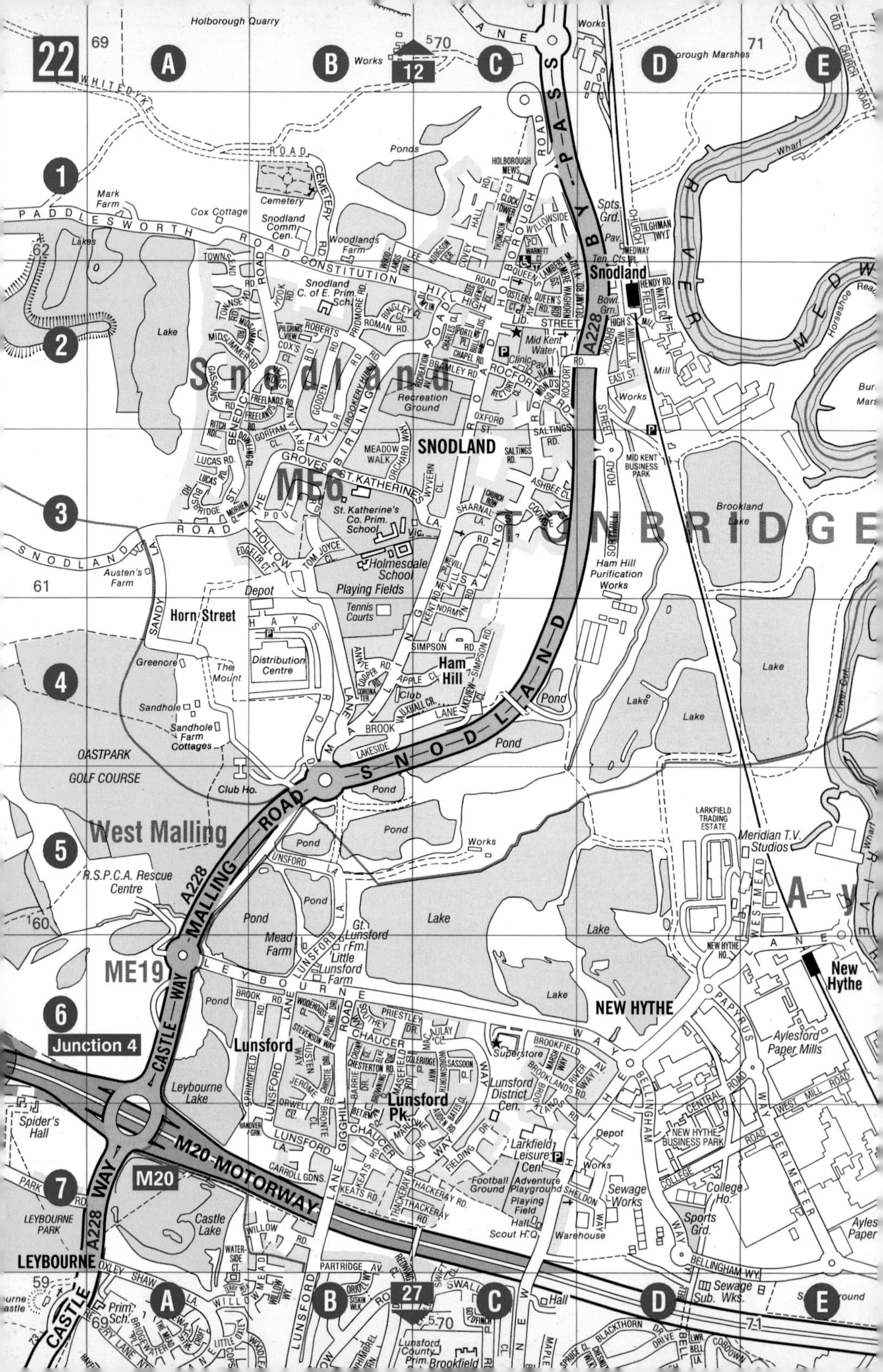
Holborough Quarry
Works
12
Holborough Marshes
OLD CHURCH ROAD
WHITEDYKE
Ponds
HOLBOROUGH MEWS
CLOCK TOWER M.
WILLOWSIDE
Spts. Grd.
Pav.
CHURCH
TILGHMAN WY.
Mark Farm
Cox Cottage
Cemetery
CEMETERY ROAD
Snodland Comm. Cen.
Woodlands Farm
PADDLESWORTH ROAD
Lakes
CONSTITUTION HILL
HIGH STREET
Snodland
HENDY RD.
FIELD
WATTS CL.
Bowl. Grn.
Lib.
Mid Kent Water
Clinic
Pav.
Snodland C. of E. Prim. Sch.
PRIDMORE RD.
BINGLEY CL.
ROMAN RD.
ROBERTS
Lake
Snodland
RECREATION AV.
BRAMLEY RD.
ROCFORT RD.
Recreation Ground
OXFORD ST.
SALTINGS RD.
SNODLAND
MEADOW WALK
ORCHARD WAY
GROVES
ST. KATHERINES LA.
WYVERN CL.
ME6
St. Katherine's Co. Prim. School
Holmesdale School
Playing Fields
Tennis Courts
TOM JOYCE CL.
BIRLING ROAD
TAYLOR
GORHAM CL.
LUCAS RD.
RITCH RD.
FREELANDS RD.
GODDEN
BENEDICT
Mill
Works
EAST ST.
MID KENT BUSINESS PARK
Brookland Lake
TONBRIDGE
Ham Hill Purification Works
SORTMILL
SNODLAND ROAD
Austen's Farm
Horn Street
SANDY LA.
Depot
HAYS ROAD
Distribution Centre
SIMPSON RD.
Ham Hill
APPLE CL.
Club
VAUXHALL CR.
LAKEVIEW CL.
BROOK LANE
LAKESIDE
Greenore
The Mount
Sandhole
Sandhole Farm Cottages
OASTPARK GOLF COURSE
Club Ho.
Pond
Lake
SNODLAND BY-PASS
A228
West Malling
MALLING ROAD
LUNSFORD LA.
Works
R.S.P.C.A. Rescue Centre
Mead Farm
Gt. Lunsford Fm.
Little Lunsford Farm
LARKFIELD TRADING ESTATE
Meridian T.V. Studios
WESTMEAD
NEW HYTHE HO.
New Hythe
ME19
LEYBOURNE
Junction 4
CASTLE WAY
Lunsford
PRIESTLEY DR.
CHAUCER WAY
SOUTHEY
Superstore
BROOKFIELD AV.
NEW HYTHE
PAPYRUS WAY
Aylesford Paper Mills
Leybourne Lake
Lunsford Pk.
Lunsford District Cen.
Spider's Hall
M20 MOTORWAY
M20
CENTRAL ROAD
WEST MILL ROAD
NEW HYTHE BUSINESS PARK
BELLINGHAM WAY
PERIMETER
COLLEGE
College Ho.
Sports Grd.
Larkfield Leisure Cen.
Football Ground
Adventure Playground
Playing Field
Hall
Scout H.Q.
Depot
Works
Sewage Works
Warehouse
Castle Lake
PARK RD.
LEYBOURNE PARK
LEYBOURNE
CARROLL GDNS.
KEATS RD.
THACKERAY RD.
PARTRIDGE AV.
OXLEY SHAW LA.
WILLOW RD.
Sewage Sub. Wks.
27
Hall
Prim. Sch.
Lunsford County Prim.
Brookfield
BLACKTHORN DR.
COBDOWN
Medway
Horseshoe Reach
Wharf
Aylesford
1
2
3
4
5
6
7
A
B
C
D
E
69
70
71
59
60
61
62

23
Burham Common
Lord Lees
Chatham
ME5
Burham Down
Rochester
ME1
and MALLING
esford
ME20
BURHAM
ECCLES
AYLESFORD
Pratling Street
Street Farm
Hall
Recn. Grnd.
Burham C.of E. Primary School
Burham C.of E. Junior School
Rose Cottage
Appledore
Petts Farm
Little Culand
Culand Cottages
Hale Farm
Hale Close
Model Cottages
Water Treatment Works
Reservoir
Rose Cottage
St. Mark's C. of E. Inf. Sch.
Recreation Ground
Sports Ground
Bushey Wood
Rowe Place Farm
Tottington Farm
Cowleaze Farm
Island Site
Sewage Wks.
CORPORATION COTTS.
Aylesford Sand & Gravel Pit.
Sand & Gravel Pit
Lodge Farm
Court Farm
Tel. Ex.
Aylesford Priory
Sports Grnd.
Community Cen.
Recn. Grnd.
Works
Depot
Warehouses
Millhall
Wharf
PILGRIMS WAY
HIGH STREET
PRATLING STREET
MEDWAY
UPPER CUT
13
24
28

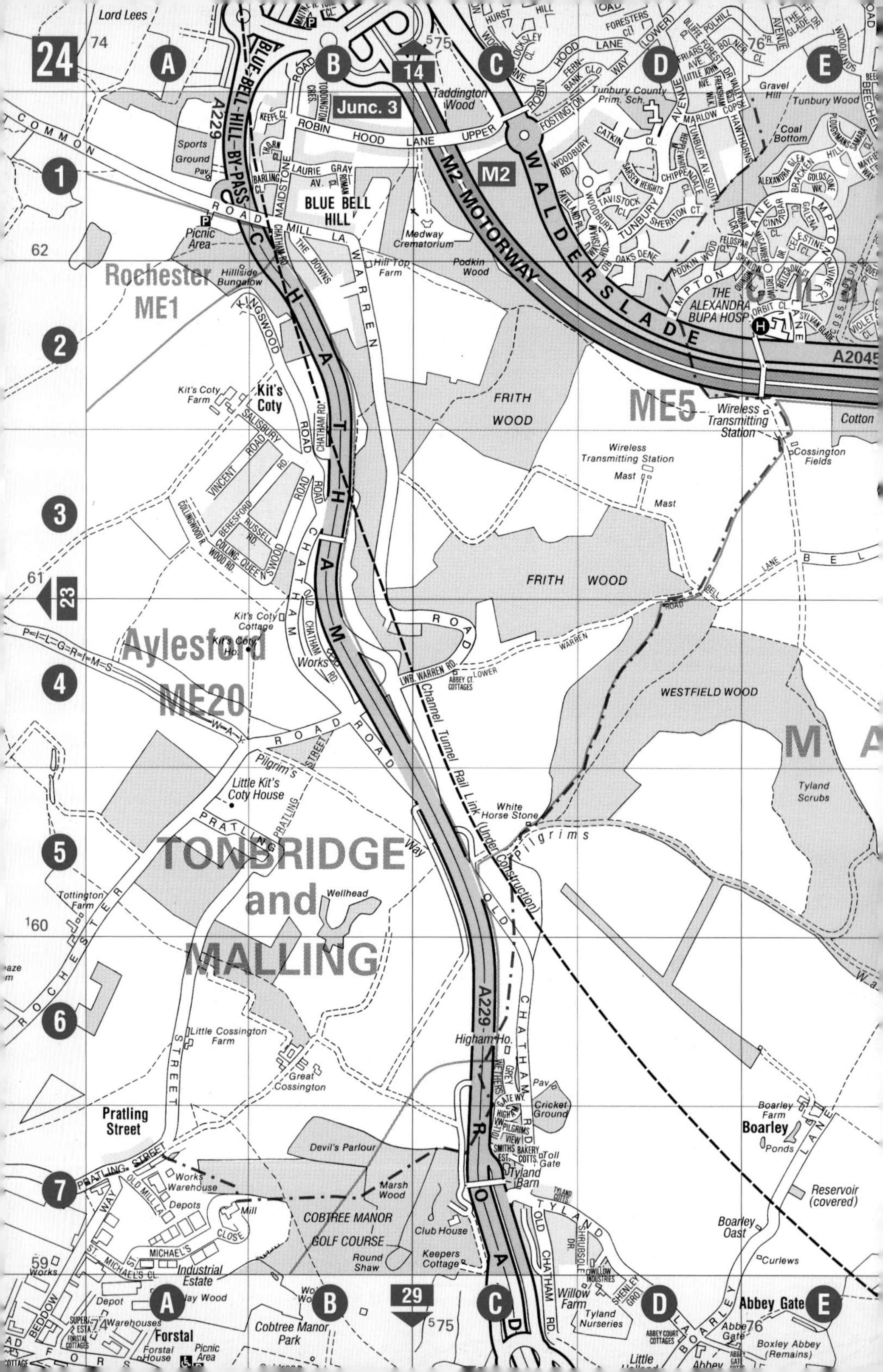
Lord Lees
74
A
B
C
D
E
575
14
Junc. 3
Taddington Wood
BLUE BELL HILL BY-PASS
A229
COMMON
ROBIN HOOD LANE UPPER
Sports Ground
Pav.
LAURIE GRAY AV.
BARLING CL.
BLUE BELL HILL
Picnic Area
ROAD
MILL LA.
Medway Crematorium
M2
M2 MOTORWAY
WALDERSLADE
Tunbury County Prim. Sch.
Tunbury Wood
Gravel Hill
Coal Bottom
TUNBURY
62
Rochester ME1
Hillside Bungalow
Hill Top Farm
Podkin Wood
THE ALEXANDRA BUPA HOSP.
A2045
CHATHAM
WARREN
KINGSWOOD
Kit's Coty Farm
Kit's Coty
FRITH WOOD
ME5
Wireless Transmitting Station
Cotton
Cossington Fields
Mast
SALISBURY ROAD
VINCENT ROAD
BERESFORD RD.
RUSSELL RD.
QUEENSWOOD
COLLINGWOOD RD.
BELL LANE
BELL ROAD
FRITH WOOD
61
23
Kit's Coty Cottage
Kit's Coty Ho.
Aylesford ME20
PILGRIMS WAY
Works
LWR. WARREN RD.
ABBEY CT. COTTAGES
WESTFIELD WOOD
Channel Tunnel Rail Link (Under Construction)
Pilgrim's Way
Little Kit's Coty House
PRATLING STREET
White Horse Stone
Pilgrims
Tyland Scrubs
TONBRIDGE and MALLING
Wellhead
Tottington Farm
ROCHESTER
60
Little Cossington Farm
Great Cossington
Higham Ho.
A229
Pav.
Cricket Ground
Pratling Street
Boarley Farm
Boarley
Ponds
Devil's Parlour
SMITHS BAKERY COTTS.
Toll Gate
Tyland Barn
Works Warehouse
Depots
Mill
OLD MILL LA.
Marsh Wood
COBTREE MANOR GOLF COURSE
Club House
TYLAND
OLD CHATHAM RD.
Reservoir (covered)
Boarley Oast
ST. MICHAEL'S CL.
Industrial Estate
Round Shaw
Keepers Cottage
Curlews
59
Works
Depot
Warehouses
29
Willow Farm
Tyland Nurseries
BOARLEY LANE
Abbey Gate
Forstal
Forstal House
Picnic Area
Cobtree Manor Park
76
Boxley Abbey (Remains)

MEDWAY
Lidsing
Gillingham
ME7
Dunn Street
Westfield Sole
MAIDSTONE
Maidstone
ME14
BOXLEY
M2 MOTORWAY
M2
WOODS
WESTFIELD
SOLE
ROAD
GLEAMING WOOD DRIVE
LORDSWOOD LANE
HARP FARM ROAD
YELSTED LANE
LIDSING ROAD
DUNN STREET
FORGE LANE
PILGRIMS WAY
BOXLEY ROAD
Swingate Co. Inf. Sch.
Spinners Acre Co. Jun. Sch.
Works
Depot
THE OAKS BUSINESS VILLAGE
ALTBARN INDUSTRIAL ESTATE
BALLARD INDUSTRIAL CENTRE
THE ENTERPRISE CENTRE
LORDSWOOD IND. EST.
Roots Wood
Sindal's Shaw
Reeds Croft Shaw
Reeds Croft Wood
Middle Field Shaw
Ivy Farm
Lidsing Court Farm
Abbey Ct. Farm
Soldiers Wood
Nurseries
Seeburg
The Cottage
Westfield Resr.
Westfield Sole Farm
Runsell Grange
Little Halstead Farm
Cuckoo Shaw
Friends Wood
MONKDOWN WOOD
BLACK COTTAGES
Boxley Grange
BOXLEY GRANGE COTTS.
Boarley Scrubs
Frogs Rough
Jubilee Bank
Boarley Warren
Harp Farm
BOXLEY WOOD
Boxley Summer House
North Downs Way
WATERWORKS COTTAGES
Water Works
Downs View Farm
Boxley House
Swimming Pool
Warren Farm
Street Farm
Church Hall
Court Lodge
Garden Lodge
Tennis Courts
The Larches
Roll Lodge
Round Wood
Westfield
15
30
F G H J K
1 2 3 4 5 6 7
77 78 79
59 60 61 62

A
B
C
D
E
1
2
3
4
5
6
7
59
158
57
56
67
68
The Old Vicarage
Church Farm
Little Ryarsh Wood
Grange Park College
Brook Farm
Sewage Works
Tennis Courts
Pavilion
Sports Ground
Audley House
Grange Park College
Leybourne Castle
LEYBOURNE PARK
LEYBOURNE
(Proposed)
Mayhill Nurseries
WEST MALLING IND. PK.
Callis Court Nurseries
LONDON ROAD
A20
A228
LEYBOURNE WOOD
Leybourne Farm
WOODS MEADOW
Callis Court Farm
Dovercourt Farm
Wingfield Bank
Redlands Farm
The Homestead
NORMAN ROAD
SANDY LANE
WEST MALLING
Village Hall
Ten. Cts.
Recreation Ground
Court Lodge
West Malling C.of E. Prim. Sch.
Cricket Ground
Day Care Cen.
Court
Tennis Court
Hermitage Farm
The Hermitage
More Park R.C. Prim. Sch.
ASHTON WAY
New Town
SWAN STREET
LUCK'S
Gatehouse
St. Mary's Abbey
Ewell Monastery
Tennis Court
TONBRIDGE
Eden Farm
West Malling for Kings Hill
Badgers Mount
Fartherwell
FARTHERWELL ROAD
ST. MARY'S CT.
Comm. Cen.
WATER LANE
Oast Houses
Three Roods
TESTON ROAD
OFFHAM ROAD
Douces Manor
Manor Farm
The Lake
Malling Place
Manor Country Park
Roman Burials Found 1892
St. Leonard's Tower
West
LAVENDERS
Spring Farm
WEST MALLING BY-PASS
Springetts Hill
Timbertops
St. Leonard's Street
Roman Burial Found 1934
EAST LAVENDERS RD.
Blaze Wood
Rathshan
St. Leonard's Farm
New Barns
ME19
Dew Pond
Oast Houses
Sportsman Farm
WINDMILL LANE CARAVAN SITE
WINDMILL LA. WEST
BROADWATER ROAD
PIKEY
St. Leonard's Wood
ASHTON WAY
ABBEY WOOD RD.
HILL
Coalpit Wood
Hoath Wood
KINGS HILL
TOWER VIEW
AVENUE
King Hill Farm
New Made Hill
KING HILL A228
MALLING ROAD
GIBSON
Coun. Offs.
KINGS
WEST MALLING
AIRFIELD
(Disused)
Works
Works
32

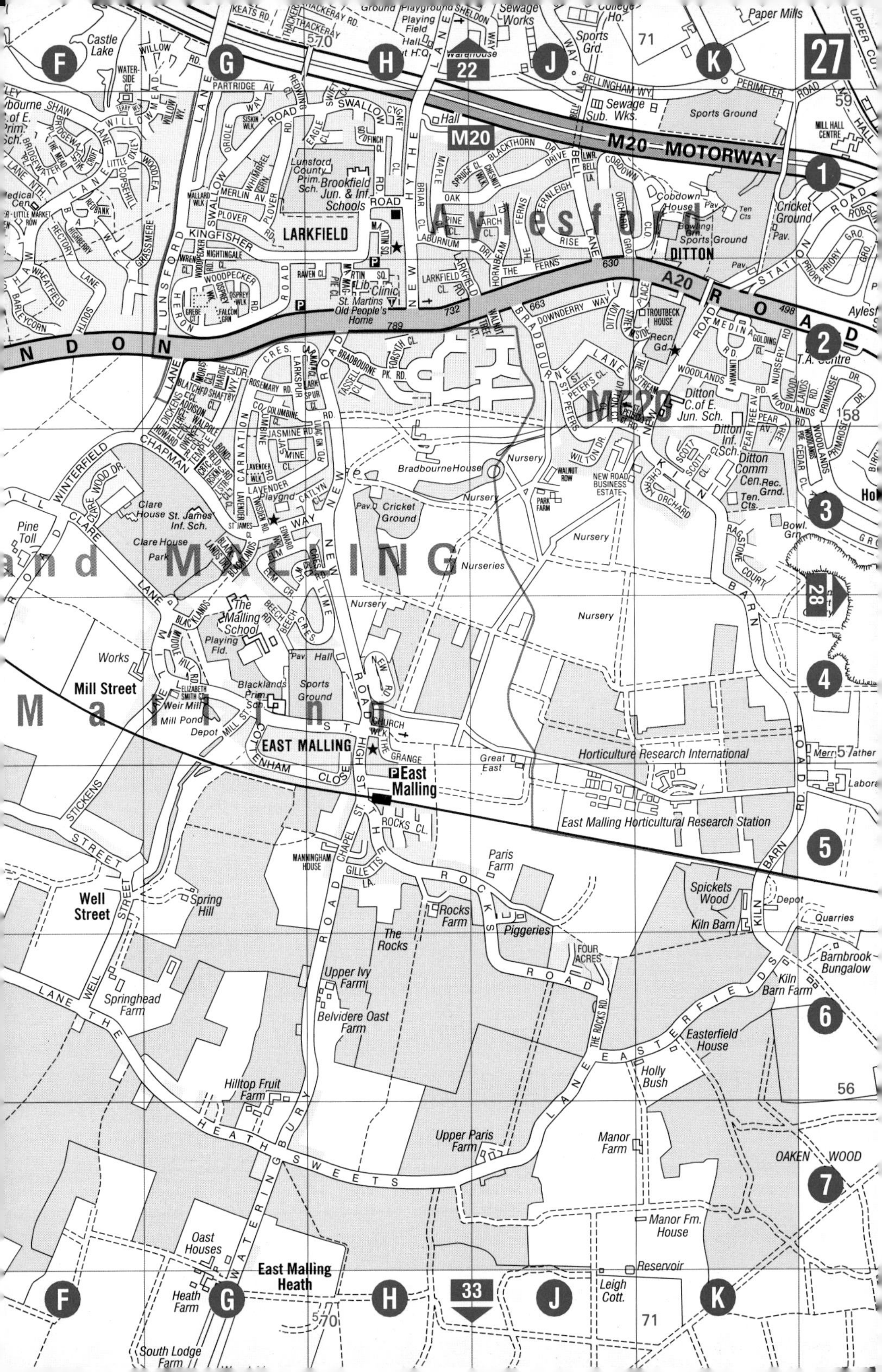
M20 MOTORWAY
A20 LONDON ROAD
Aylesford
LARKFIELD
DITTON
East MALLING
EAST MALLING
East Malling
Mill Street
Well Street
East Malling Heath
Horticulture Research International
East Malling Horticultural Research Station
Lunsford County Prim. Sch.
Brookfield Jun. & Inf. Schools
The Malling School
Blacklands Prim. Sch.
Clare House Park
Bradbourne House
Castle Lake
Paper Mills
Sports Ground
Cricket Ground
Spickets Wood
Kiln Barn
Kiln Barn Farm
Barnbrook Bungalow
Easterfield House
Holly Bush
Manor Farm
Manor Fm. House
Reservoir
Leigh Cott.
Oaken Wood
Upper Paris Farm
Paris Farm
Rocks Farm
The Rocks
Piggeries
Four Acres
Upper Ivy Farm
Belvidere Oast Farm
Hilltop Fruit Farm
Springhead Farm
Spring Hill
Oast Houses
Heath Farm
South Lodge Farm
Manningham House
Pine Toll
Works
Weir Mill
Mill Pond
Depot
Nursery
Nurseries
22
28
33

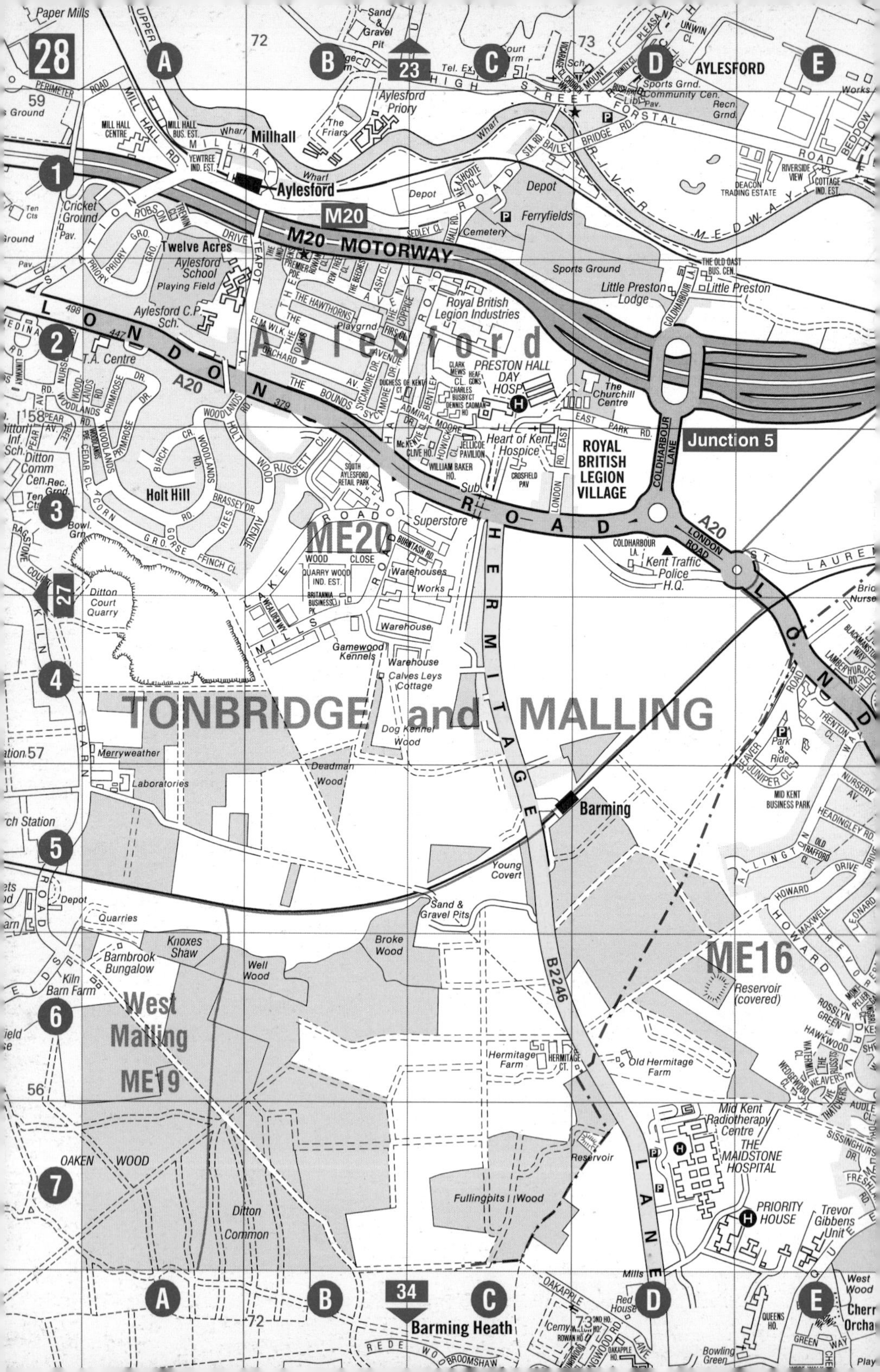

A
B
C
D
E
1
2
3
4
5
6
7
72
73
59
58
57
56
23
27
34
Paper Mills
Sand & Gravel Pit
Aylesford Priory
The Friars
AYLESFORD
HIGH STREET
Sports Grnd.
Community Cen.
Recn. Grnd.
FORSTAL RD.
BAILEY BRIDGE RD.
RIVER MEDWAY
Millhall
MILL HALL RD
MILL HALL CENTRE
MILL HALL BUS. EST.
YEWTREE IND. EST.
Aylesford
M20
M20 MOTORWAY
Depot
Ferryfields
Cemetery
Sports Ground
Little Preston Lodge
Little Preston
THE OLD OAST BUS. CEN.
RIVERSIDE VIEW
DEACON TRADING ESTATE
COTTAGE IND. EST.
Cricket Ground
Twelve Acres
Aylesford School Playing Field
Aylesford C.P. Sch.
Royal British Legion Industries
Aylesford
PRESTON HALL DAY HOSP.
The Churchill Centre
EAST PARK RD.
Junction 5
COLDHARBOUR LANE
Heart of Kent Hospice
ROYAL BRITISH LEGION VILLAGE
LONDON ROAD
A20
Holt Hill
T.A. Centre
Ditton Inf. Sch.
Ditton Comm Cen.
Rec. Grnd.
SOUTH AYLESFORD RETAIL PARK
Superstore
ME20
QUARRY WOOD IND. EST.
BRITANNIA BUSINESS PK
Warehouses
Works
Warehouse
Gamewood Kennels
Calves Leys Cottage
Ditton Court Quarry
Kent Traffic Police H.Q.
TONBRIDGE and MALLING
Dog Kennel Wood
Deadman Wood
Merryweather Laboratories
HERMITAGE LANE
B2246
Barming
Young Covert
Sand & Gravel Pits
Quarries
Knoxes Shaw
Well Wood
Broke Wood
Barnbrook Bungalow
Kiln Barn Farm
West Malling ME19
ME16
Reservoir (covered)
Hermitage Farm
Old Hermitage Farm
Mid Kent Radiotherapy Centre
THE MAIDSTONE HOSPITAL
Reservoir
Fullingpits Wood
Ditton Common
OAKEN WOOD
PRIORITY HOUSE
Trevor Gibbens Unit
Park & Ride
MID KENT BUSINESS PARK
Barming Heath
Red House
West Wood

Junction 6
M20 MOTORWAY
M20
COBTREE MANOR GOLF COURSE
Cobtree Manor Park
Forstal
Abbey Gate
Boxley Abbey (Remains)
Sandling
ME14
MAIDSTONE
Maidstone
Allington
Ringlestone
Invicta Park
H.M.P. Maidstone
Maidstone East
Maidstone Barracks
MAIDSTONE
Maidstone West
Museum of Kent Life
Allington Castle
Castle Quarries (Disused)
Proposed Channel Tunnel Rail Link
ROYAL ENGINEERS ROAD
A229 ROAD
FAIRMEADOW
A20
HIGH ST.
KING ST.
24
30
35

A
B
C
D
E
1
2
3
4
5
6
7
25
29
36
BOXLEY
Boxley House
Swimming
PILGRIMS WAY
Warren Farm
THE STREET
Street Farm
Church Hall
Court Lodge
Garden Lodge
Tennis Courts
Lark Rise
Park Croft
Park House
Roll Lodge Shaw
The Larches
Hillside
Nine Acre Shaw
Donkey Shaws
Park Wood
Weir
Ponds
Blacklands Shaw
Cooks Cottage
GRANGE LANE
Cope Hill Shaw
Yewtree Shaw
East Lodge
Harpole
HARPLE LANE
Channel Tunnel Rail Link (Under Construction)
Harbourlands Farm
Stonehouse
M20
Harbourland
Park Wood
Dove Hill
Dovehill Wood
BOXLEY ROAD
SANDY LANE
Sandling Prim. Sch.
Beulah Wood
The Old Workhouse
MAID
Maid
M20 MOTORWAY
Hockers Shaw
Kiln Wood
Works
Club
Tennis Courts
Junction 7
Pond
SITTINGBOURNE ROAD
A249
Horish Wood
SANDLING LANE
Recreation Ground
Penenden Heath
Heath Wood
Rose Cottage
PENENDEN HEATH ROAD
Newnham Court
Horish Wood
Works
Stakis Country Court Hotel
HEATHFIELD ROAD
Gallows Hill
R.C.Inf. & Prim. Schs.
BEARSTEAD RD.
Garden Centre
The Chimneys
Carlaw
Tall Trees
Lower Fullingpits Wood
Vinters Park Crematorium
BEARSTED ROAD
Pope's Wood
Grove Wood
Television Studios
VINTERS PARK
Works
GROVEWOOD DRIVE
Wents Wood
East Lodge
THE MINOR CENTRE
Superstore
Comm. Cen.
Med. Cen.
Grove Green
Vinters Valley Nature Reserve
Grove Lodge
Depot
Playing Field
St. John's C. of E. Prim. Sch.
NEW CUT ROAD
Invicta Grammar Sch.
Vinters Boys School
HOLLAND RD.
Sittingbourne Rd. Cen.
E. Borough C. P. Sch.
Sports Ground
ASHFORD ROAD
A20
ME15
MAIDSTONE
River Len
WAT TYLER WY
Fish Pond
Model Track
Miniature Railway
Boat House
Cricket Ground
Rugby
LORD ROMNEY'S HILL
MEADOW WLK.
77
78
59
158
57
56

F
G
H
J
K
Norton Farm
SCRAGGED OAK CARAVAN PARK
Kent County Show Ground
Highland Grange
59
Clear View
BROADER LANE
SCRAGGED OAK RD.
Mill Cottages
Murrain Place
Penny Spring
Millfield
Candy Cott.
SITTINGBOURNE ROAD
A249
Reed Wood
Byeways
Wild Air
Hillcrest
Gorse Tor Farm
OSBOURNE DRIVE
Cottage Wood
DETLING HILL
Friningham
Lynch Bank
The Lynch
Little Upfield
ROAD
DETLING
EAST COURT COTTAGES
PILGRIMS WAY
CIVILEY WOOD
Godard's or Thurnham Castle (rems.)
Red Pike
The Croft
Croftside
DETLING
Hog Trough Bottom
158
Castle Cottages
Thurnham Keep
THURNHAM
Works
Hockers Farm
Pilgrims Nurseries
The Friars
Yewtree Shaw
Fox Fm. Cotts.
Little Dane
ALDINGTON LANE
COLDBLOW LANE
Thurnham Court
Ten. Ct.
The Cottage
Cricket Ground
Aldington Court Farm Cottages
Home Meadow Plantation
Thurnham Keep Farm
Cobham Manor
Court Farm
Cobham Oast House
ME14
Corbier Hall Wood
Gore Wood Farm
57
Honeyhills Wood
Gore Wood
Channel Tunnel Rail Link (Under Construction)
The Basin
Bar Meadow Shaw
Clayswood
BEARSTED GOLF COURSE
Longham Wood
Chapel Lane Farm
Ponds
The Cottage
Fairways
M20 MOTORWAY
Ware Street
Depot
Club House
Bearsted
Green Pastures
WATER LANE
THURNHAM LANE
56
Pumping Station
Hog Hill
Snowfield
Bridge Farm
Poer Meadow Shaw
Subway
M20
Lodge
St. Faith's Home
Eylesden Court School
Barty Farm
Thurnham C of E. Inf. & Roseacre Jun. Schs.
Roseacre
Bertie Ho.
The Belt
Tennis Cts.
Playing
Mote House
Common Wood
Crismill Shaw
Bowling Green
37
Gore Cottage
Commonwood
80
81
Major's Wood
BEARSTED
Nursery

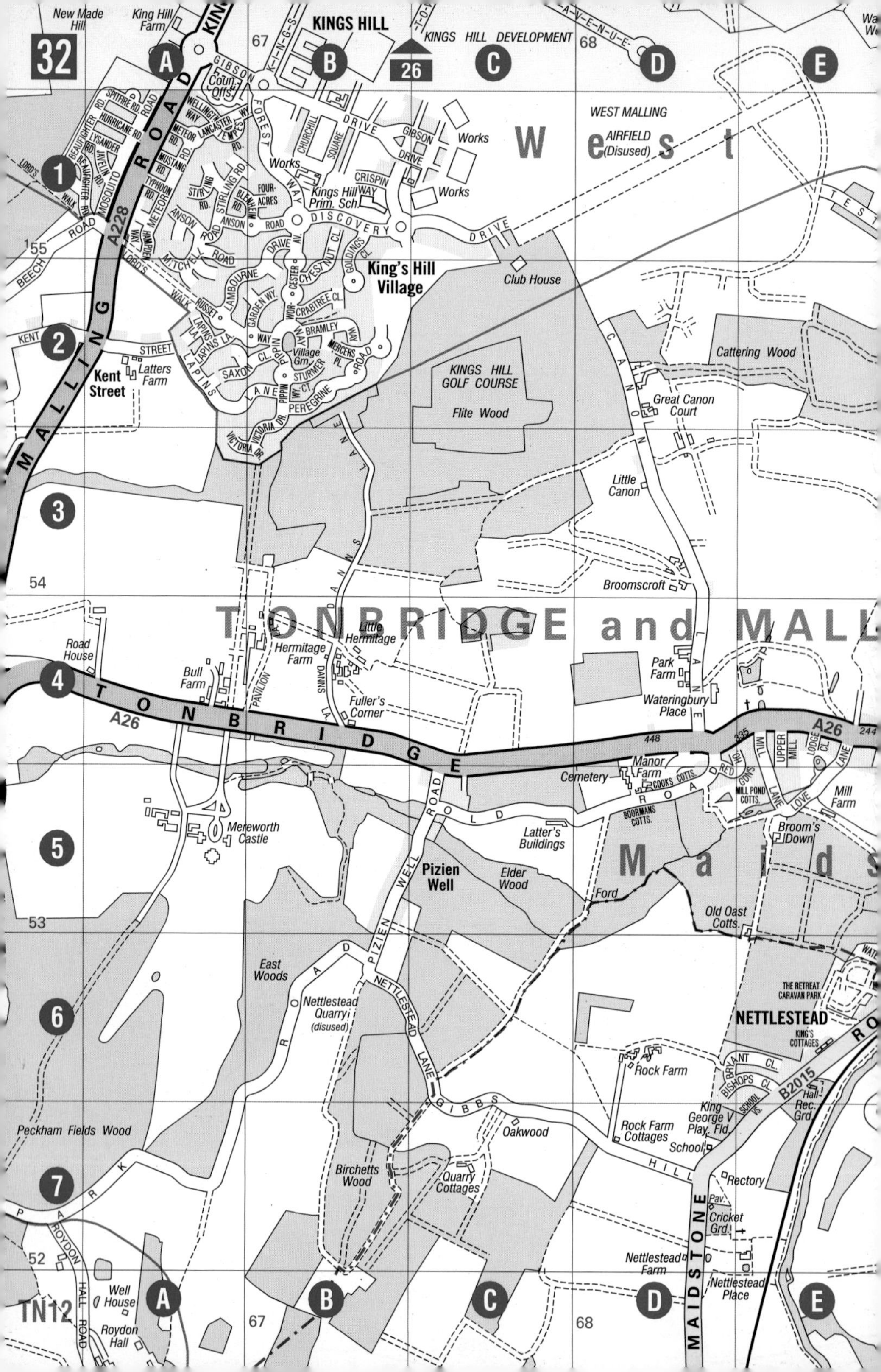

New Made Hill
King Hill Farm
KINGS HILL
KINGS HILL DEVELOPMENT
26
A
B
C
D
E
67
68
Coun. Offs.
GIBSON
K-I-N-G-S
A-V-E-N-U-E
WEST MALLING
AIRFIELD (Disused)
W e s t
SPITFIRE RD.
HURRICANE RD.
BEAUFIGHTER RD.
LYSANDER
JAVELIN RD.
MOSQUITO
WELLINGTON WAY
LANCASTER
TEMPEST WY.
METEOR RD.
MUSTANG RD.
TYPHOON RD.
STIRLING RD.
BLENHEIM RD.
FOUR-ACRES
ANSON RD.
ANSON ROAD
MITCHELL ROAD
HAMPDEN WAY
LORD'S WALK
FOREST WAY
CHURCHILL SQUARE
DRIVE
GIBSON DRIVE
CRISPIN WAY
Works
Kings Hill Prim. Sch.
DISCOVERY
DRIVE
GOLDINGS CL.
CHESTNUT CL.
WORCESTER AV.
LAMBOURNE DRIVE
GARDEN WY.
CRABTREE CL.
King's Hill Village
Club House
TESTON
1
2
3
4
5
6
7
155
54
53
52
A228
MALLING ROAD
BEECH ROAD
KENT STREET
Kent Street
Latters Farm
RUSSET
LAPINS LA.
LAPINS LANE
SAXON CL.
PIPPIN WAY
Village Grn.
BRAMLEY WAY
STURMER CT.
MERCERS PL.
ROAD
PEREGRINE
PIPPIN WY.
VICTORIA DR.
KINGS HILL GOLF COURSE
Flite Wood
CANON LANE
Cattering Wood
Great Canon Court
Little Canon
Broomscroft
DANNS LANE
TONBRIDGE and MALL
Little Hermitage
Hermitage Farm
Road House
Bull Farm
PAVILION
DANNS LA.
Fuller's Corner
Park Farm
Wateringbury Place
A26
TONBRIDGE ROAD
448
335
244
Manor Farm
Cemetery
COOKS COTTS.
RED HILL
GUNS
OLD ROAD
MILL POND COTTS.
MILL LANE
UPPER MILL
LODGE CL.
LANE
LOVE
Mill Farm
BOORMANS COTTS.
Latter's Buildings
Broom's Down
Mereworth Castle
Pizien Well
ROAD
Elder Wood
Ford
M a i d s
Old Oast Cotts.
PIZIEN WELL
East Woods
ROAD
Nettlestead Quarry (disused)
NETTLESTEAD LANE
THE RETREAT CARAVAN PARK
NETTLESTEAD
KING'S COTTAGES
BRYANT CL.
BISHOPS CL.
SCHOOL VS.
B2015
Rock Farm
King George V Play. Fld.
Hall
Rec. Grd.
Peckham Fields Wood
GIBBS HILL
Oakwood
Rock Farm Cottages
School
Birchetts Wood
Quarry Cottages
Rectory
PARK
Pav.
Cricket Grd.
ROYDON HALL ROAD
Nettlestead Farm
MAIDSTONE
Nettlestead Place
Well House
Roydon Hall
TN12

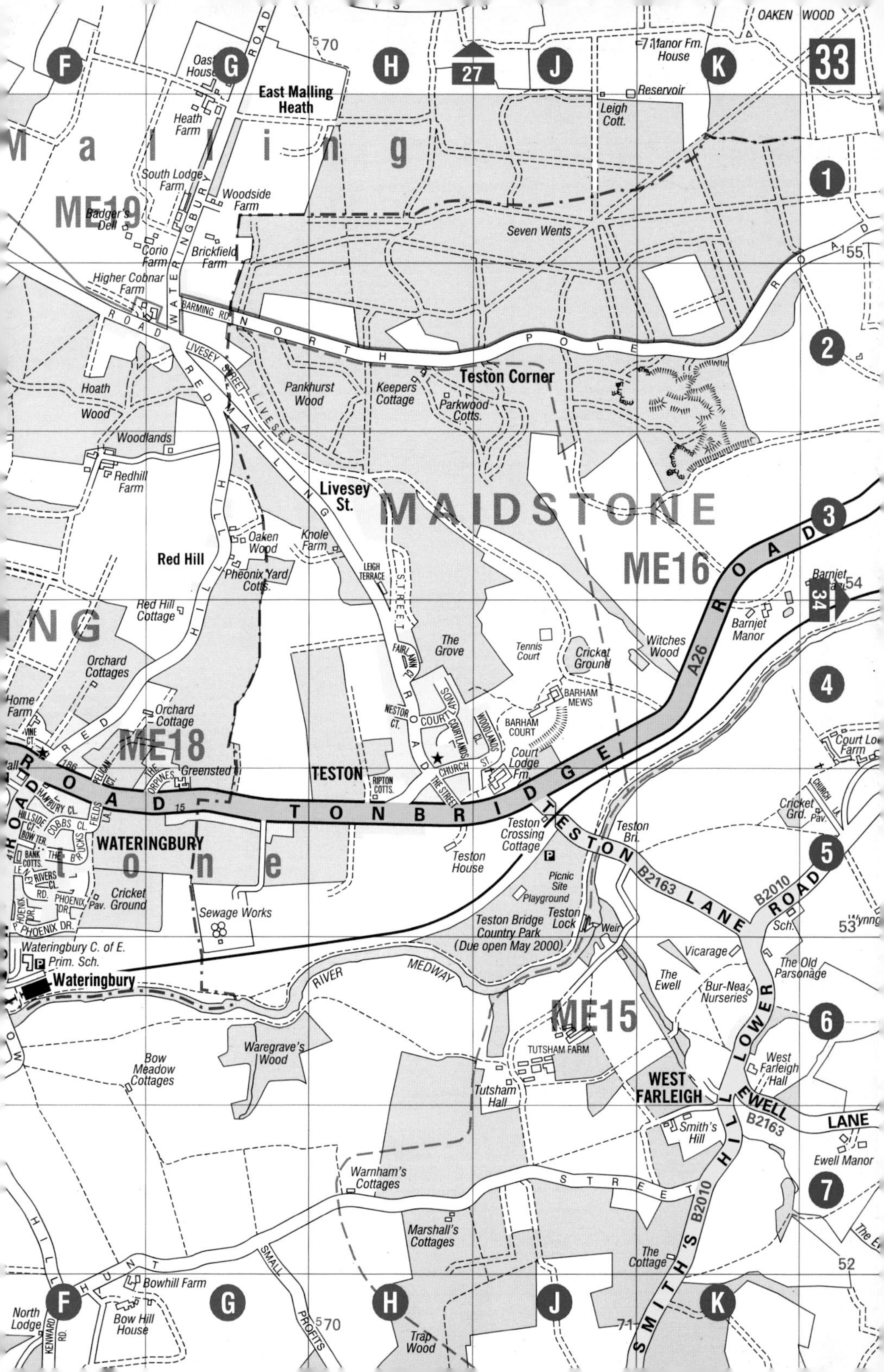
27
34
OAKEN WOOD
Manor Fm. House
Reservoir
Oast House
East Malling Heath
Heath Farm
Leigh Cott.
Malling
South Lodge Farm
Woodside Farm
ME19
Badger's Dell
Seven Wents
Corio Farm
Brickfield Farm
Higher Cobnar Farm
WATERINGBURY ROAD
BARMING RD.
NORTH POLE ROAD
LIVESEY STREET
Teston Corner
Hoath Wood
Pankhurst Wood
Keepers Cottage
Parkwood Cotts.
RED HILL
RED MALLING
Woodlands
Redhill Farm
Livesey St.
MAIDSTONE
Oaken Wood
Knole Farm
Red Hill
Pheonix Yard Cotts.
LEIGH TERRACE
STREET
ME16
A26
ROAD
Barnjet Manor
Red Hill Cottage
The Grove
Tennis Court
Cricket Ground
Witches Wood
Orchard Cottages
FAIRLAWN CL.
Home Farm
Orchard Cottage
NESTOR CT.
COURT LANDS
COURTLANDS
WOODLANDS CL.
BARHAM MEWS
BARHAM COURT
Court Lodge Farm
VINE CT.
ME18
PELICAN CT.
THE ORPINES
Greensted
TESTON
RIPTON COTTS.
CHURCH ST.
THE STREET
Court Lodge Fm.
CHURCH LA.
Cricket Grd.
Pav.
TONBRIDGE ROAD
HAMBURY CL.
HILLSIDE CT.
COBBS CL.
BOW TER.
FIELDS LA.
BANK COTTS.
BUCKS
WATERINGBURY
LENEY RD.
RIVERS CL.
PHOENIX DR.
Cricket Ground
Pav.
Sewage Works
Wateringbury C. of E. Prim. Sch.
Wateringbury
TESTON
Teston Crossing Cottage
Teston House
Teston Bri.
B2163 LANE
B2010
LOWER ROAD
Picnic Site
Playground
Teston Lock
Weir
Teston Bridge Country Park (Due open May 2000)
Sch.
Vicarage
The Old Parsonage
RIVER MEDWAY
The Ewell
Bur-Nea Nurseries
ME15
Waregrave's Wood
TUTSHAM FARM
West Farleigh Hall
Bow Meadow Cottages
Tutsham Hall
WEST FARLEIGH
EWELL LANE
B2163
Smith's Hill
Ewell Manor
Warnham's Cottages
STREET
Marshall's Cottages
The Cottage
SMITH'S HILL B2010
HILL
HUNT
SMALL PROFITS
Bowhill Farm
North Lodge
KENWARD RD.
Bow Hill House
Trap Wood
F
G
H
J
K
1
2
3
4
5
6
7
570
71
55
54
53
52
186
15

OAKEN WOOD
Ditton Common
Fullingpits Wood
28
PRIORITY HOUSE
Trevor Gibbens Unit
ME19
Barming Heath
HERMITAGE LA.
B2246
POLE ROAD
NORTH POLE ROAD
REDE WOOD RD.
BROOMSHAW RD.
ROBERTS ORCHARD RD.
BEECHWOOD RD.
WESLEY CL.
NORTH STREET
HEATH ROAD
Hall Place Swimming Pool
Hall Place Farm
The Lodge
Bowling Green
St. Andrews House
Blackthorn Centre
Transport Depot
Prim. Sch.
Recn. Grnd.
A26
TONBRIDGE ROAD
BARMING
Barming County Prim. Sch.
Bell Fm.
BULL ORCHARD
War Mem.
PRIORS DEAN CL.
School Recreation Ground
CHURCH LANE
Court Lodge
Barnjet Cottage
Barnjet Manor
33
ME16
GLEBE LANE
Glebe Farm
GATLAND LANE
Gatling Cottages
MAIDSTONE
RECTORY LANE
Homewood
Old Rectory Bungalow
Old Rectory
The Oast House
Bridge Cottage
Works
RIVER MEDWAY
Barming Bridge
Riverdale
ST. HELENS LANE
Prospect Place
Half Yoke Farm
Wood Cottages
Scraces
Beckett's Place
Piggeries
East Farleigh
Jupesa
West Lo
Court Lodge Farm
Hopper's Corner
Warf Cottage
Lock
B2010
Kettle Corner
St. Helen's
Lower Gallants Farm
Oaklands
Little Adelaide Farm
East Farleigh Bridge
Cricket Grd.
Pav.
CHARLTON LANE
Hillcroft
Kettle Farm
Hoplands
The Cottage
LOWER ROAD
FORGE
Library
EAST FARLEIGH
Sch.
Wynngarth
Gallants Court
Gallants Bungalow
VICARAGE LANE
The Old Parsonage
Elmscroft
Elmscroft Farm
Five Oasts
Cokehurst
Playing Field
Willow Wood
Park Cottage
Gallants Manor
East Farleigh C.P. School
The Oast
Farleigh Green
The Vicarage
West Farleigh Hall
Parsonage Cottages
Gallants Farm
Cedarwood House
EWELL LANE
B2163
KETTLE LANE
GALLANTS LANE
Ewell Manor
Furminger Cottages
HEATH ROAD
Castle Acre
The Ewell
Inglewood
Moon's Farm
Roses Farm
Highland Farm
The Thatched House
Hospital Barn Farm
Cuckoo Farm
WILSONS LANE
QUARRY WOOD
40
Castle Farm
Love's Cottage
DEAN
PLEASANT
52
53
54
55
72
73
A B C D E
1 2 3 4 5 6 7

35
F
G
H
J
K
29
36
41
1
2
3
4
5
6
7
155
54
53
52
575
76
ME15
MAIDSTONE
Maidstone West
Fant
Tovil
Dean Street
LOOSE
Oakwood Park
Kent Institute of Art & Design
Oakwood Farm
The Astor of Hever Sch.
The Poplars Nursing Home
Oakwood Park Grammar Sch.
Westboro' Sports Cen.
Clare Recn. Grnd.
Ten. Cts. & Bowl. Greens
TONBRIDGE RD.
A26
B2010
A229
FANT LANE
UPPER FANT RD.
MEDWAY
Bydews Wood
Bydews Place
Bydews Farm
Fant Farm
Fant House
Lone Cottage
East Lodge
Dean Farm
Valley Farm
Munsfield Oast
Court Lodge Farm
Bungalow Farm
Gate House Farm
Rockwell Farm
Cull's Farm
Malthouse Cottages
Frith Hall
Hamlet Wood
Stonecroft
Stone Cottage
Sewage Works
The Wool Ho.
Pimp's Court
Tennis Courts
Windy Ridge
Loose Hill
Loose Court Farm
Loose Court Farm Cottage
Old Loose Court
Limekiln Shaw
Loose Valley
Abbey Gate Place
Abbey Gate Farm
Little Abbey Gate Farm
Abbey Gate Cottages
Little Abbey Gate
Tovil Mill
County Fire H.Q.
Cricket Ground
Mill Pond
Up. Crisbrook Cotts.
Hayle Place
Waste Disposal Site
Farleigh Hill Retail Pk.
Tovil Green Business Park
Farleigh Trad. Est.
Postley Industrial Centre
Fountain Enterprise Park
Park & Ride
South Park
South Park Business Village
Armstrong Halls
Sports Ground
Loose Bowls Club
Y Sports Centre
Fire Brigade Training Cen.
Loose Cty. Infant & Junior Schs.
King George V Playing Field
Merriehills
Maidstone Grammar Sch.
Collis Mem. Gnd.
The Palace
Mus.
Crown Ct.
Market Pl. Park & Ride
Cattle Mkt.
Boro' Offs.
Offices
Depot
Works
FARLEIGH HILL
DEAN STREET
DEAN ROAD
STOCKETT LANE
BUSBRIDGE LANE
NEW CUT
CRIPPLE STREET
LOOSE ROAD
LINTON ROAD
HAYLE RD.
COLLEGE RD.
UPPER STONE ST.
KNIGHTRIDER ST.
SHEAL'S CR.
TOVIL ROAD
TOVIL HILL
POSTLEY ROAD
ARMSTRONG RD.
CAVE HILL
BOCKINGFORD LA.
TEASAUCER HILL
VALE ROAD
SALTS LANE
Linden Farm
Forstal Farm
Quarry Wood

36
MAIDSTONE
ASHFORD RD.
A20
30
35
42
ME15
ME17
MOTE PARK
Mote Park Leisure Centre
Indoor Bowls Centre
Cricket Ground
Mote Cricket Club Ground
Rugby Grd.
Rugby Ground
Playground
Boat House
Yacht Sta.
Fish Pond
Miniature Golf Course
Model Car Racing Track
Miniature Railway
Raigersfeld
Turkey Mill
Vinters Boys School
Mote House
Tennis Ct.
Weir
River Len
Park & Ride
Otham Lodge
Mote Cott.
Cobtree Hall
Church Lodge
Keepers Cottage
Downswood
MAIDS
Willington
Maid
Rectory
Church Cottages
Maidstone Grammar Sch. Playing Field
Park Way Co. Prim. Sch.
South Park
LOOSE ROAD
A229
A274
SUTTON ROAD
Shepway
Club Pavilion
Shepway Cty. Jun. & Inf. Schs.
Recreation Ground
Molehill Copse Community Clinic
Molehill Copse Prim. Sch.
Kent County Constabulary Headquarters
Sports Ground
Superstore
Senacre Technical College
Playing Field
Senacre Wood
Senacre Wood Co. Prim. Sch.
Mangravet
Mangravet Wood
Maidstone Cemetery
Fire Brigade Training Cen.
Oldborough Manor Comm. Sch.
Five Acre Wood Sch.
Five Acre Wood
Tennis Cts.
Works
Police Training School
Boughton Mount
Boughton Mount Farm
Lockham
Merriehills
Quarry Wood
The Quarries
Park Wood
Bell Wood Schs. & Woodside Cen.
Convent
R.C. Prim. Sch.
Spectrum Business Estate
Wren Industrial Estate
Haslemere Estate
Loose Bowls Club
Sports Centre
Armstrong Halls
Bowling Grns.
Tennis Cts.
Prim. Sch.
A B C D E
1 2 3 4 5 6 7
77 78
52 53 54 55

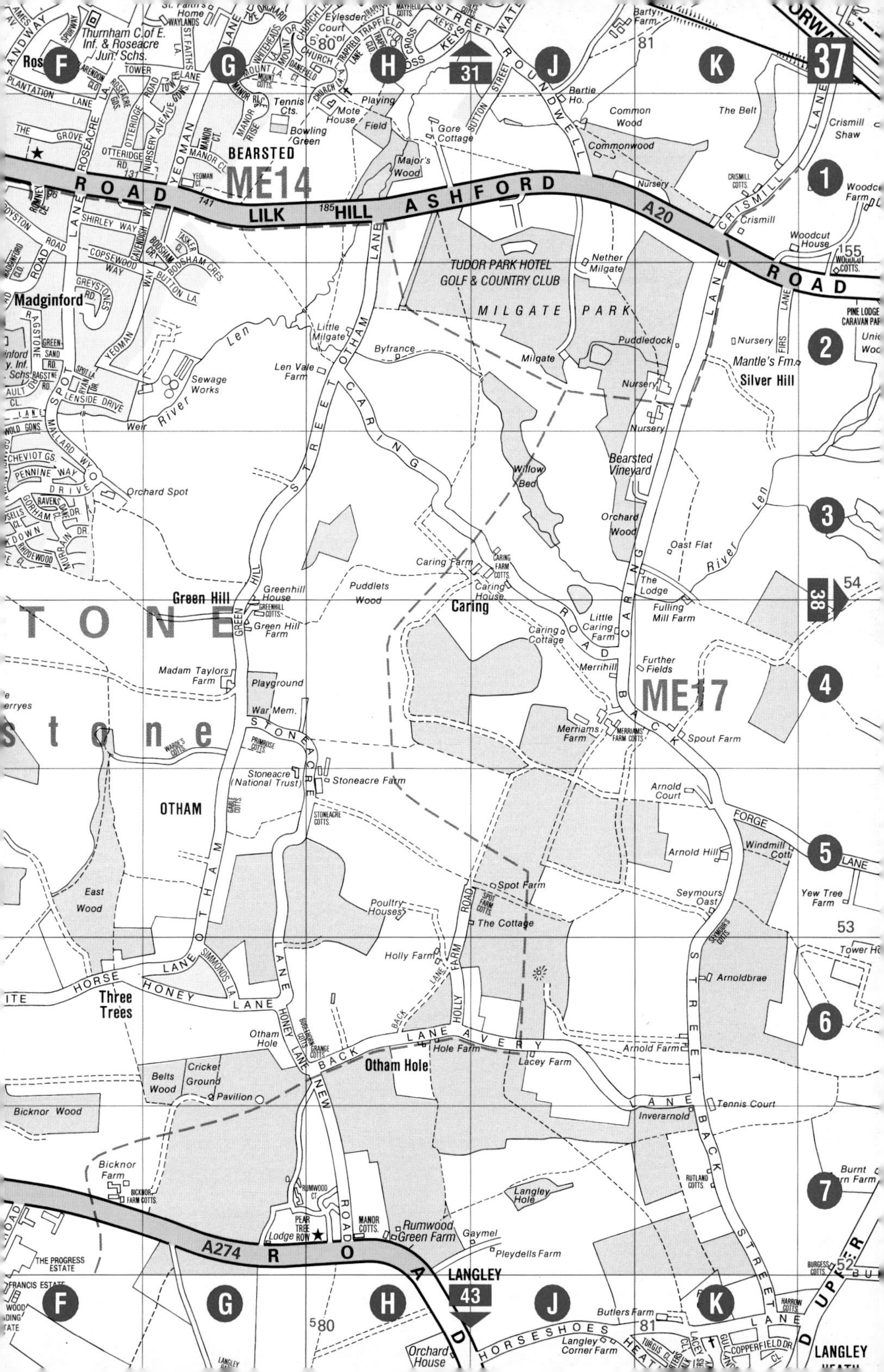

37
31
38
43
F
G
H
J
K
1
2
3
4
5
6
7
ME14
ME17
BEARSTED
Madginford
Thurnham C. of E. Inf. & Roseacre Jun. Schs.
TUDOR PARK HOTEL GOLF & COUNTRY CLUB
MILGATE PARK
Milgate
Silver Hill
Caring
Green Hill
OTHAM
Three Trees
Otham Hole
LANGLEY
LANGLEY HEATH
ASHFORD ROAD
LILK HILL
A20
A274
Bearsted Vineyard
Sewage Works
Common Wood
The Belt
Crismill Shaw
Crismill
Nether Milgate
Puddledock
Mantle's Fm.
Nursery
Willow Bed
Orchard Wood
Oast Flat
River Len
Little Milgate
Byfrance
Len Vale Farm
Caring Farm
Caring House
Puddlets Wood
Greenhill House
Green Hill Farm
Madam Taylors Farm
Playground
War Mem.
Stoneacre (National Trust)
Stoneacre Farm
East Wood
Poultry Houses
Holly Farm
Spot Farm
The Cottage
Merriams Farm
Spout Farm
Arnold Court
Arnold Hill
Seymours Oast
Arnoldbrae
Arnold Farm
Tennis Court
Inverarnold
Hole Farm
Lacey Farm
Belts Wood
Cricket Ground
Pavilion
Bicknor Wood
Bicknor Farm
Langley Hole
Rumwood Green Farm
Gaymel
Pleydells Farm
Butlers Farm
Langley Corner Farm
Orchard House
THE PROGRESS ESTATE
Orchard Spot
Fulling Mill Farm
Further Fields
The Lodge
Little Caring Farm
Caring Cottage
Merrihill
Windmill Cott
Yew Tree Farm
Woodcut House
Gore Cottage
Major's Wood
Bowling Green
Tennis Cts.
Playing Field
Mote House
Bertie Ho.
Barty Farm
Commonwood

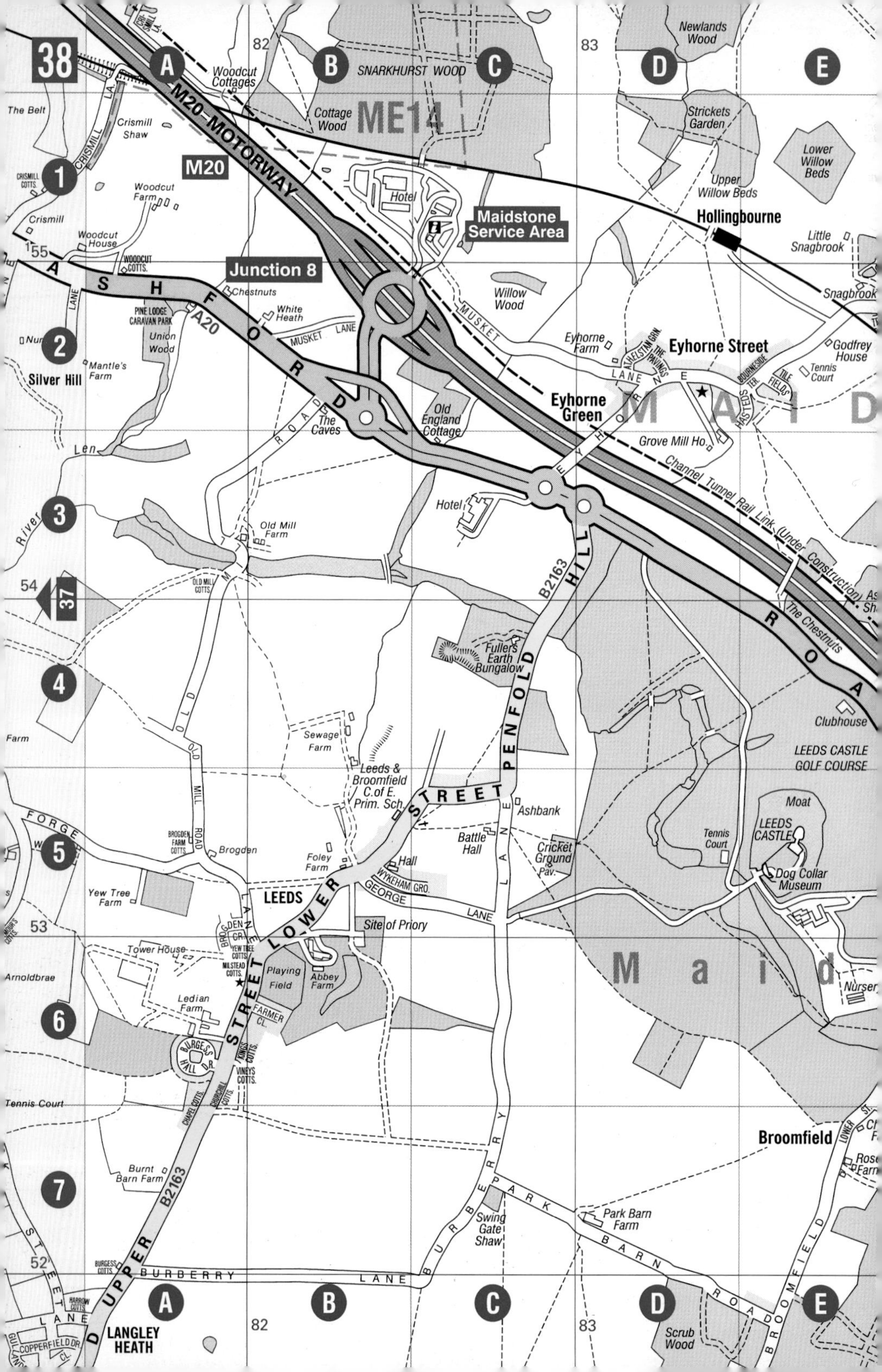
A
B
C
D
E
1
2
3
4
5
6
7
82
83
55
54
53
52
37
Woodcut Cottages
SNARKHURST WOOD
Newlands Wood
The Belt
Crismill Shaw
Cottage Wood
ME14
Strickets Garden
Lower Willow Beds
M20
M20 MOTORWAY
CRISMILL LA.
CRISMILL COTTS.
Crismill
Woodcut Farm
Hotel
Upper Willow Beds
Maidstone Service Area
Hollingbourne
Woodcut House
WOODCUT COTTS.
Junction 8
Little Snagbrook
ASHFORD ROAD
A20
Chestnuts
White Heath
PINE LODGE CARAVAN PARK
Union Wood
Willow Wood
Snagbrook
MUSKET LANE
Eyhorne Farm
Eyhorne Street
Godfrey House
Silver Hill
Mantle's Farm
Tennis Court
Eyhorne Green
The Caves
Old England Cottage
Grove Mill Ho.
Len
Channel Tunnel Rail Link (Under Construction)
River
Hotel
Old Mill Farm
OLD MILL COTTS.
B2163
HILL
The Chestnuts
Fullers Earth Bungalow
Clubhouse
Farm
Sewage Farm
LEEDS CASTLE GOLF COURSE
OLD MILL ROAD
PENFOLD
Leeds & Broomfield C.of E. Prim. Sch.
STREET
Moat
Ashbank
LEEDS CASTLE
Battle Hall
Tennis Court
FORGE
BROGDEN FARM COTTS.
Brogden
Foley Farm
Hall
Cricket Ground Pav.
Dog Collar Museum
Yew Tree Farm
LEEDS
WYKEHAM GRO.
GEORGE LANE
LOWER STREET
Site of Priory
Tower House
YEW TREE COTTS.
MILSTEAD COTTS.
Playing Field
Abbey Farm
Maid
Arnoldbrae
Ledian Farm
FARMER CL.
Nursery
BURGESS HALL DR.
KINGS COTTS.
VINEYS COTTS.
Tennis Court
CHAPEL COTTS.
CHURCHILL COTTS.
Broomfield
Burnt Barn Farm
BURBERRY LANE
Swing Gate Shaw
PARK BARN ROAD
Park Barn Farm
BROOMFIELD ROAD
STREET
UPPER STREET
BURGESS COTTS.
HARROW COTTS.
LANGLEY HEATH
Scrub Wood
COPPERFIELD DR.
GULAND CL.

HOLLINGBOURNE
Manor House
Vicarage
Cricket Ground
Pav.
Frogshole
The Warren
High Wood
Salisbury Wood
Clifford's Shaw
DRAKE LANE
PILGRIMS WAY
HOLLINGBOURNE HILL
UPPER ST.
GREENWAY
Oak Meadow Farm
STONE
Willow Bed
Target
Five Arch Bridge
COURT ROAD
Pilgrims Way
Strake's Wood
Mile Hill
Greenway Court Farm
Greenway Court
Harpswood
Harps Wood
Warren Wood House
Warren Wood
HOSPITAL ROAD
Snyden Pond
COURT LODGE RD.
COURT LODGE COTTAGES
Hamilton Springs
Goddington Wood
Goddington
The Ruffetts
Mount Farm
Greenway Forstal
GREENWAY
ME17
THE GARDEN OF ENGLAND MOBILE HOME PARK
Penn Lodge
Oaklea
Swim. Pool
Ockley Mead
Holme Lodge
Harrietsham
HARRIETSHAM
Holm Mill
HOLM MILL LA.
Home Lake
Park Wood
Parkwood Farm
Piggery
WEST STREET
STATION RD.
ASHFORD ROAD
A20 ROAD
M20 MOTORWAY
M20
CHEGWORTH ROAD
Chegworth
CHEGWORTH MILL COTTAGES
WATER LANE
Waterlane Farm
Little Chegworth
Ashen Wood
Chegworth Court
Pollhill
Pollhill Mill
River Len
Lenhurst
Rumchild
Spion Kop Farm
Poplar Farm
Sewage Works
FAIRBOURNE LANE
Cherry Gardens
Mill House
Fairbourne Mill
HOOK LA.
QUESTED WY.
WENS WY.
CRICKETERS CL.
FORGE MDW.
WEST ST.
BUCKINGHAM GDNS.
TEN ACRE CT.
F G H J K
1 2 3 4 5 6 7
585 86 155 54 53 52

34
A
B
C
D
E
1
2
3
4
5
6
7
52
51
50
49
72
73
QUARRY WOOD
Fox Pitt
Downs Farm Cottages
SHINGLE BARN LANE
Greybury Wood
Buston Manor Farm
Oast Houses
Malice Wood
Poundfield Shaw
LUGHORSE LANE
Little Filers Wood
Obelisk House
Park House
The Thatched House
Castle Acre
Love's Cottage
The Retreat
Hilltop Place
JEFFRIES COTTAGES
HILLTOP
UPPER HEATH ROAD
Keepers Cottage
HEATH
B2163
Castle Farm
Pike Wood
BARN HILL
BARN HILL COTTS
Barn Hill
Barn Hill Farm
ME15
NEW COTTS
Reservoirs
Tennis Ct.
Leylands
Gennings Farm
Forge Cottage
HUNTON
EAST STREET
North Lodge
Playing Field
Pav.
Cricket Grd.
Bowl Green
Hall
Grave Yard
HUNTON
Southover
GROVE LANE
Grove Farm
THE SQUARE
BENSTED CL.
South Lodge
Hunton C. of E. Prim. Sch.
WEST STREET
PEACE COTTAGES
BISHOP'S LANE
Durrants
Durrant's Farm
Oak Cottage
Bishops House
Bishop's Oast
Water Place
LANE
WATER LANE
Forsters Cottage
Elphick's Farm
Shepherds Cottages
River Beult
Inglewood
Highland Farm
Hospital Barn Farm
GALLANTS LANE
WILSONS LANE
Cuckoo Farm
COUNCIL COTTAGES
CRITTENDEN COTTAGES
Crittenden Bungalows
WALLERS COTTAGES
ASHDOWNS COTTAGES
North Folly Farm
Woodville
Folly Hatch
NORTH FOLLY ROAD
FOREMANS BARN RD
Coxheath Nursery
Horse Shoe Farm
UPPER HUNTON HILL
THE WENTS
Enclosures
AMSBURY RD
Amsbury Wood
Hillside Cottage
Amsbury Croft
MAIDS
Maids
Amsbury Oast
Old Savage
Weald Cottage
Tennis Ct.
Reason Hill
PLEASANT
ADBERT DR.
FAIRHURST DR.
Yelton
WHITEBEAM DR.
WOODLANDS
PIPPIN CL.
HUNTINGTON
DEAN STREET
Rectory
Hunton Court Farm
Court Lodge
Hunton Court
The Elms
Elm Corner
Works
Foresters Cottage
The Stores
Hunton Place
Clock House
STREET
WALL
Brickyard Cotts.
Martins Cottages
Martins Farm House
Marchcroft
Stonewall
Burford Farm
Burford Farm Cottages
Stonewall Oast House
EAST GEORGE STREET
Clapper House
Bridge House
Clapper Green
HUNTON ROAD
Reed Court Farm Trail
Tonbridge
TN12

COXHEATH
Linden Farm
Forstal Farm
Sewage Works
Salts Farm
Filmer's Farm
Campfield
Haste Hill
Heath Farm
BOUGHTON MONCHELSEA
Heathside Ho. Day Centre
Coxheath C.P. Sch.
Coxheath Cen.
HEATH ROAD
B2163
LINTON HILL
A229
The Cornwallis Sch.
Playing Fields
Kent Fire Brigade Training Centre
Reservoir (covered)
Cricket Ground
Clock House Farm
TONE
tone
Southwards
Hill House Farm
LINTON PARK
Court Lodge
Maytum Farm
Home Farm
Village Hall
Linton
Snoads Hall
Toke Place
Toke Farm
Swim. Pool
The White Lodge
Pitts Farmhouse
ME17
Barns Cottages
Old South Lodge
Playground
The Forge
The White House
Loddington Farm
The Acorns
Wares Farm
Brick Kiln Wood
Shibbler Shaw
Redwall Farmhouse
Redwall Farm
Sewage Farm
Redwall Plantation
Reservoir
Depot
River Farm
The Bungalow
Ware Farm
BUTT GREEN LANE
Ranter's Plantation
Rankins Farm Cottages
Rankins Farm
Davis Cottages
White House Farm
STILEBRIDGE LANE
42
35

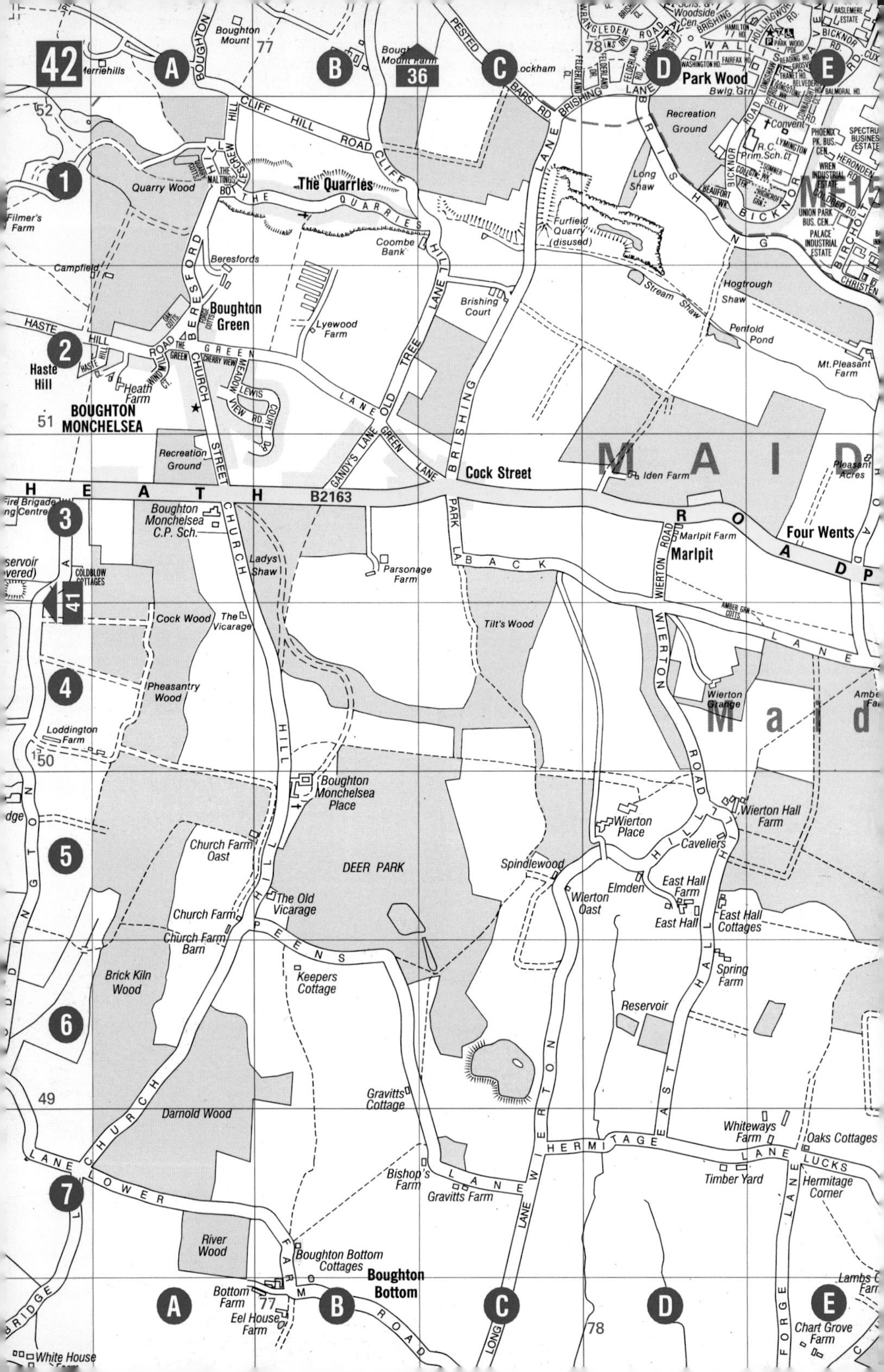

36
41
Boughton Mount
Merriehills
Bought Mount Farm
Park Wood
Recreation Ground
Quarry Wood
The Quarries
Filmer's Farm
The Maltings
Coombe Bank
Furfield Quarry (disused)
Long Shaw
Beresfords
Campfield
Boughton Green
Lyewood Farm
Brishing Court
Stream Shaw
Hogtrough Shaw
Penfold Pond
Mt.Pleasant Farm
Haste Hill
Heath Farm
BOUGHTON MONCHELSEA
Recreation Ground
Cock Street
Iden Farm
MAID
Pleasant Acres
HEATH ROAD
B2163
Fire Brigade Centre
Boughton Monchelsea C.P. Sch.
Ladys Shaw
Parsonage Farm
Marlpit Farm
Marlpit
Four Wents
Coldblow Cottages
Cock Wood
The Vicarage
Tilt's Wood
Amber Grn Cotts
Wierton Grange
Maid
Pheasantry Wood
Loddington Farm
Boughton Monchelsea Place
Wierton Place
Wierton Hall Farm
Church Farm Oast
DEER PARK
Spindlewood
Caveliers
Elmden
East Hall Farm
Wierton Oast
East Hall
East Hall Cottages
The Old Vicarage
Church Farm
Church Farm Barn
Keepers Cottage
Spring Farm
Brick Kiln Wood
Reservoir
Gravitts Cottage
Darnold Wood
Whiteways Farm
Oaks Cottages
Hermitage Lane
Timber Yard
Hermitage Corner
Bishop's Farm
Gravitts Farm
Lucks Lane
River Wood
Boughton Bottom Cottages
Boughton Bottom
Bottom Farm
Eel House Farm
Lambs Cross Farm
Chart Grove Farm
White House
Lower Lane
Church Hill
Peens Lane
Wierton Lane
Long Lane
Forge Lane
Farm Road
Wierton Road
Back Lane
Park La
Brishing Lane
Old Tree Lane
Green Lane
Gandy's Lane
Church Street
Beresford Road
Cliff Hill Road
The Quarries
Quarries Hill
Pested Bars Rd.
Haste Hill Road
Green Lane
Meadow View Rd.
Lewis Court Dr.
Cherry View
Loddington
Bridge
Wierton Hill
East Hall Hill
Bicknor Road
Brishing Road
Wallis Av
A B C D E
1 2 3 4 5 6 7
77 78
49 50 51 52

SUTTON ROAD
37
LANGLEY
Langley Hole
Rumwood Green Farm
Pleydells
Lodge Row
PEAR TREE ROW
MANOR COTTS.
RUMWOOD CT.
BICKNOR FARM COTTS.
Butlers Farm
Rec. Grd.
BACK STREET
HARROW COTTS.
UPPER
HORSESHOES LANE
Langley Corner Farm
LANGLEY HEATH
Orchard House
Elmhurst
Langley Park Farm
LANGLEY PARK FARM COTTS.
STONE COTTS.
TURGIS CL.
PORTERS WALK
LACEY CL.
GULLANDS
COPPERFIELD DR.
DICKENS CL.
SKINNERS WY.
FORSTERS
SHEPHERDS WY.
ORCHARD CL.
HEATH ROAD
HEATH FIELD
GRASSLANDS
GREEN LA. COTTS.
Green La. Farm
GREEN LANE
B2163
ULCOMBE ROAD
GRAVELLY BOTTOM RD.
PITT RD.
Langley Loch
SUTTON ROAD
A274
Rectory Farm
Hall
Wild Oaks
PLOUGH COTTS.
LEEDS ROAD
ABBEY WOOD
S T O N E
LESTED LANE
Pleasant Farm
Five Wents
COLLINGWOOD INDUSTRIAL CENTRE
Oakdenne Farm
MAIDSTONE ROAD
WEST VIEW COTTS.
Firtree Farm
CHART SUTTON BUSINESS ESTATE
New House Farm
Valleta
Lested Farm
WENTS ROAD
NORTON ROAD
Filter Bed
COBFIELD
LAXTON DR.
B2163
AMBER WAY
Chart Corner
WARMLAKE INDUSTRIAL ESTATE
AMBERFIELD COTTS.
ORCHARD BANK
WARMLAKE LANE
Thatch House
Norton Pond
Warmlake
Warmlake
STREET
MARSHAM CR.
Recreation Ground
Norton Ct.
Norton Forstal
ROAD
CHARTWAY
MERCER WY.
Hall
CHART SUTTON
Playing Field
Vanguard Farm
50
ME17
ALMERY COTTS.
Ambercourt
Sports Ground
Newlyns
High Cote
Haven Farm
Rec. Ground
Hall
Pleasant Field Bungalow
Ladds Ct. Farm
Ladds Ct.
CHURCH ROAD
Sports Ground
Sports Ground
Underhill Jun. Sch.
Court Farm
SOUTH WAYS
Underhill House
Sutton Valence County Prim. Sch.
Ten. Cts.
SUTTON VALENCE
CHART
Chart Mill
Heronden
Res.
Sutton Valence Sch.
SCHOOL LA.
Sch.
Castle View
Manor Farm
HIGH STREET
BROAD ST.
TUMBLERS HILL
LOWER ROAD
RECTORY
CHAPEL RD.
Hall
THE PLATT
LANE
NORTH STREET
Sutton Platt Cottage
SOUTH BANK
Park House Farm
Rectory Farm
RECTORY LANE
Priory House
Coombe Farm
Little Belringham
Hollingworth Hall
49
Sutton Place
South Orchard
Southfields Stables
Place Wood
(SUTTON VALENCE WAY)
HEADCORN ROAD
A274
Noons Farm
CAPTAIN'S CL.
SOUTH LANE
The Harbour
THE HARBR.
Forsham Cottages
FORSHAM LANE
Hall
Sparks Farm
Forsham Farm
Brookside
580
81
F
G
H
J
K
1
2
3
4
5
6
7

INDEX TO STREETS

Including Industrial Estates and a selection of Subsidiary Addresses.

HOW TO USE THIS INDEX

1. Each street name is followed by its Postal District and then by its map reference; e.g. Abbey Rd. *Roch* —7H **3** is in the Rochester Posttown and is to be found in square 7H on page **3**.
   A strict alphabetical order is followed in which Av., Rd., St., etc. (though abbreviated) are read in full and as part of the street name; e.g. Apple Clo. appears after Appleby Clo. but before Appledore Ct.

2. Streets and a selection of Subsidiary names not shown on the Maps, appear in the index in *Italics* with the thoroughfare to which it is connected shown in brackets; e.g. *Aintree Ho. Maid —6E **36** (off Epsom Clo.)*

GENERAL ABBREVIATIONS

All : Alley
App : Approach
Arc : Arcade
Av : Avenue
Bk : Back
Boulevd : Boulevard
Bri : Bridge
B'way : Broadway
Bldgs : Buildings
Bus : Business
Cvn : Caravan
Cen : Centre
Chu : Church
Chyd : Churchyard
Circ : Circle
Cir : Circus
Clo : Close
Comn : Common
Cotts : Cottages
Ct : Court
Cres : Crescent
Dri : Drive
E : East
Embkmt : Embankment
Est : Estate
Gdns : Gardens
Ga : Gate
Gt : Great
Grn : Green
Gro : Grove
Ho : House
Ind : Industrial
Junct : Junction
La : Lane
Lit : Little
Lwr : Lower
Mnr : Manor
Mans : Mansions
Mkt : Market
M : Mews
Mt : Mount
N : North
Pal : Palace
Pde : Parade
Pk : Park
Pas : Passage
Pl : Place
Quad : Quadrant
Rd : Road
Shop : Shopping
S : South
Sq : Square
Sta : Station
St : Street
Ter : Terrace
Trad : Trading
Up : Upper
Vs : Villas
Wlk : Walk
W : West
Yd : Yard

POSTTOWN AND POSTAL LOCALITY ABBREVIATIONS

All : Allington
Ayle : Aylesford
Bap : Bapchild
Barm : Barming
Bear : Bearsted
Blue B : Blue Bell Hill
Bob : Bobbing
B'den : Borden
Bou M : Boughton Monchelsea
Boxl : Boxley
Bred : Bredhurst
Bromp : Brompton
Broom : Broomfield
Burh : Burham
Cha S : Chart Sutton
Chat : Chatham
Chatt : Chattenden
Cli : Cliffe
Cox : Coxheath
Cux : Cuxton
Det : Detling
Dit : Ditton
Down : Downswood
E Far : East Farleigh
E Mal : East Malling
E Peck : East Peckham
Eccl : Eccles
Gill : Gillingham
Gill B : Gillingham Bus. Pk.
Hall : Halling
H'shm : Harrietsham
H'lip : Hartlip
Hem : Hempstead
High : Higham
Holl : Hollingbourne
Hoo : Hoo
Hunt : Hunton
Iwade : Iwade
Kem : Kemsley
King H : Kings Hill
Kgswd : Kingswood
Langl : Langley
Lark : Larkfield
Leeds : Leeds
Leyb : Leybourne
Lin : Linton
Loose : Loose
Lwr Hal : Lower Halstow
Lwr U : Lower Upnor
Maid : Maidstone
Mere : Mereworth
Mil R : Milton Regis
Murs : Murston
Nett : Nettlestead
N'tn : Newington
Otham : Otham
Quar W : Quarry Wood
Rain : Rainham
Roch : Rochester
Roy B : Royal British Legion Village
Rya : Ryarsh
St Mi : St Marys Island
S'lng : Sandling
Shorne : Shorne
Sit : Sittingbourne
Snod : Snodland
S'bry : Stockbury
Strood : Strood
Sut V : Sutton Valence
Tstn : Teston
T'hm : Thurnham
Tonge : Tonge
Tovil : Tovil
Upc : Upchurch
Upnor : Upnor
Up H'lng : Upper Halling
Wain : Wainscott
W'slde : Walderslade
W'bury : Wateringbury
Weav : Weavering
W Far : West Farleigh
W Mal : West Malling
W'sham : Windlesham
Woul : Wouldham
Yald : Yalding

INDEX TO STREETS

Austell Mnr. Gill —2G 9
(off Skinner St.)
Austen Way. Lark —6B 22
Austin Clo. Kem —1E 20
Autumn Glade. Chat —2H 25
Aveling Clo. Hoo —1H 5
Aveling Ct. Roch —1K 7
Avenue of Rememberance. Sit —6C 20
Avenue, The. Ayle —2B 28
Averenches Rd. Bear —6E 30
Averenches Rd. S. Bear —7E 30
Avery Clo. Maid —3J 35
Avery La. Otham —6J 37
Aviemore Gdns. Bear —7E 30
Avington Clo. Maid —3J 35
Avocet Wlk. Chat —7G 15
Avondale Rd. Gill —3H 9
Avon Ho. Maid —4D 36
Aylesford Cres. Gill —5B 10
Aylewyn Gn. Kem —1D 20

Backfields. Roch —4K 7
Back La. Cha S —3C 42
Back La. Maid —6H 37
Back St. Leeds —4J 37
Baden Rd. Gill —1H 9
Bader Cres. Chat —2E 14
Badger Rd. Chat —1G 25
Baffin Clo. Chat —6D 8
Bailey Bri. Rd. Ayle —1C 28
Bailey Ct. Gill —1A 16
Bailey Dri. Gill B —7A 10
Bakenham Ho. Roch —7A 8
Baker La. Sut V —6K 43
Baker St. Burh —1H 23
Baker St. Roch —5A 8
Bakers Wlk. Roch —2A 8
Bakery Cotts. S'lng —7C 24
Balfour Rd. Chat —6C 8
Ballard Bus. Pk. Roch —3H 7
Ballard Ind. Est. Chat —2G 25
Ballens Rd. Chat —6F 15
Balls Ct. Chatt —3D 4
Balmer Clo. Gill —2D 16
Balmoral Ho. Maid —7E 36
Balmoral Rd. Gill —3G 9
Balmoral Ter. Sit —5B 20
Bangor Rd. Roch —2F 7
Bank Cotts. Holl —1F 39
Bankfields Clo. Gill —7H 11
Banks Cotts. W'bury —5F 33
Bankside. Chat —1F 15
Banks Rd. Roch —7A 4
Bank St. Chat —5F 9
Bank St. Maid —7J 29
Banky Meadow. Maid —1C 34
Banning St. Roch —7K 3
Bannister Hill. B'den —7K 19
Bannister Rd. Maid —4K 29
Barbados Ter. Maid —4K 29
Barberry Av. Chat —4B 14
Barcham Ct. Maid —7J 35
Bardell Ter. Roch —3B 8
Barden Ct. Maid —6A 30
Barfleur Mnr. Gill —2E 8
(off Middle St.)
Barfreston Clo. Maid —2J 35
Bargrove Rd. Maid —6B 30
Barham Clo. Maid —7D 36
Barham Ct. Tstn —4J 33
Barham M. Tstn —4J 33
Barker Rd. Maid —1J 35
Barkers Ct. Sit —5B 20
Barkis Clo. Roch —2B 14
Barleycorn. Leyb —2F 27
Barleycorn Dri. Gill —3E 16
Barleyfields. Weav —7C 30
Barleymow Clo. Chat —3G 15
Barling Clo. Chat —1B 24
Barlow Clo. Gill —4E 16
Barming Pl. Maid —2C 34
Barming Rd. W'bury —2G 33
Barnaby Ter. Roch —6A 8
Barnard Ct. Chat —6E 8
Barn Clo. B'den —7J 19
Barncroft Clo. Weav —7E 30
Barncroft Dri. Hem —5K 15
Barndale Ct. Shorne —4A 2
Barned Ct. Maid —2C 34
Barnes La. Lin —5F 41
Barnfield. Chat —1E 14
Barn Hill. Hunt —4B 40
Barn Hill Cotts. Maid —2C 40
Barnhurst Rd. Maid —3K 29
Barn Meadow. Up H'lng —5A 12
Barnsole Rd. Gill —3H 9
Barnwood Clo. Roch —1K 13

Baron Clo. Bear —6E 30
Baron Clo. Gill —1J 9
Barrie Dri. Lark —6B 22
Barrier R. Chat —3D 8
Barrington Clo. Chat —4D 14
Barrowfields. Chat —1H 25
Barrow Gro. Sit —6B 20
Bartlett Clo. Chat —1G 25
Barton Rd. Maid —2K 35
Barton Rd. Roch —1J 7
Basi Clo. Roch —6A 4
Basing Clo. Maid —1A 36
Basmere Clo. Maid —5B 30
Bassett Rd. Sit —5B 20
Batchelor St. Chat —4E 8
Bates Clo. Lark —7C 22
Bath Hard. Roch —3B 8
Bayford Rd. Sit —5E 20
Bayswater Dri. Gill —5E 16
Baywell. Leyb —1F 27
Beacon Clo. Gill —2D 16
Beacon Hill. Chat —7G 9
Beacon Hill La. Chatt —3D 4
Beacon Rd. Chat —6G 9
Beaconsfield Av. Gill —3J 9
Beaconsfield Rd. Chat —6D 8
Beaconsfield Rd. Maid —2H 35
Beaconsfield Rd. Sit —6G 21
Beacons, The. Cox —3F 41
Beams, The. Maid —3D 36
Bearstead Rd. Maid —4B 30
Bearsted Clo. Gill —5B 10
Bearsted Grn. Bus. Cen. Bear —7H 31
Beatty Av. Gill —5K 9
Beatty Rd. Roch —1B 14
Beaufighter Rd. W Mal —1A 32
Beaufort Ct. Roch —2C 8
Beaufort Pk. Roch —3C 8
Beaufort Rd. Roch —6G 3
Beaufort Wlk. Maid —1D 42
Beaulieu Rise. Roch —7B 8
Beaulieu Wlk. Maid —4F 29
Beaumont Rd. Maid —2E 34
Beauvoir Dri. Kem —1E 20
Beauworth Pk. Maid —4D 36
Beaver Rd. Maid —4E 28
Beckenham Dri. Maid —4G 29
Beckenham Pk. Gill —5J 11
Beckley M. Chat —4D 14
Becksbourne Clo. Maid —3K 29
Beckworth Pl. Maid —1E 34
Beddow Way. Ayle —1E 28
Bedford Av. Gill —7D 10
Bedford Pl. Maid —7H 29
Bedgebury Clo. Maid —5B 30
Bedgebury Clo. Roch —1B 14
Bedson Wlk. Gill —7H 11
Bedwin Clo. Roch —2B 14
Beech Dri. Maid —6F 29
Beechen Bank Rd. Chat —7E 14
Beeches, The. Ayle —2B 28
Beeches, The. Chat —5E 14
Beech Gro. High —4D 2
Beech Hurst Clo. Maid —2A 36
Beeching Rd. Chat —6F 15
Beechings Grn. Gill —5C 10
Beechings Ind. Cen. Gill —4B 10
Beechings Way. Gill —4B 10
Beechmore Dri. Chat —7E 14
Beech Rd. E Mal —4G 27
Beech Rd. Mere —2A 32
Beech Rd. Roch —2H 7
Beechwood Av. Chat —6H 9
Beechwood Av. Sit —3C 20
Beechwood Rd. Maid —1C 34
Begonia Av. Gill —6C 10
Beke Rd. Gill —5D 16
Belfast Ho. Maid —5D 36
Belgrave Ho. Roch —1K 7
Belgrave St. Eccl —4H 23
Bell Cres. Burh —2H 23
Bellgrove Ct. Chat —2E 24
Bellingham Way. Lark & Ayle —6D 22
Bell La. Boxl —6F 31
Bell La. Burh —2H 23
Bell La. Chat —3D 24
Bell La. Dit —1J 27
(in two parts)
Bellmeadow. Maid —6D 36
Bell Rd. Maid —6D 36
Bell Rd. Sit —7C 20
Bell Shop. Cen., The. Sit —5D 20
Bell's La. Hoo —1H 5
Belmont Clo. Maid —2C 34
Belmont Rd. Gill —4G 9
Belmont Rd. Sit —6C 20

Belnor Av. Bob —1G 19
Belvedere Ho. Maid —7E 36
Bendon Way. Gill —1D 16
Benedict Clo. Hall —5D 12
Benenden Mnr. Gill —5B 10
Benenden Rd. Wain —5A 4
Bennetts Cotts. Gill —2K 25
Bensted Clo. Hunt —6A 40
Bentley Clo. Chat —7H 15
Bentley Clo. Roy B —2C 28
Bentlif Clo. Maid —6G 29
Berber Rd. Roch —7K 3
Berengrave La. Gill —7E 10
Beresford Av. Chat —6C 8
Beresford Hill. Bou M —2A 42
Beresford Rd. Ayle —3A 24
Beresford Rd. Gill —4H 9
Bergland Pk. Roch —7B 4
Berkeley Clo. Roch —1B 14
Berkeley Ct. Sit —6B 20
Berkeley Mt. Chat —4D 8
Berkshire Clo. Chat —1G 15
Berry St. Sit —5D 20
Berwyn Gro. Maid —6K 35
Best St. Chat —4D 8
Bethersden Ct. Maid —5E 36
Betjeman Clo. Lark —7B 22
Betony Gdns. Weav —6E 30
Betsham Rd. Maid —6E 36
Bettscombe Rd. Gill —2D 16
Beverley Clo. Gill —1F 17
Beverley Rd. Maid —2C 34
Bicknor Farm Cotts. Langl —7F 37
Bicknor Rd. Maid —7E 36
Biddenden Clo. Bear —1E 36
Bilberry Clo. Weav —6D 30
Bill St. Rd. Roch —6A 4
Bilsington Clo. Chat —4F 15
Bingham Rd. Roch —6A 4
Bingley Rd. Snod —2B 22
Binland Gro. Chat —4B 14
Binnacle Rd. Roch —1A 14
Birch Cres. Ayle —3A 28
Birch Dri. Chat —1H 25
Birchfield Clo. Maid —6A 36
Birchfields. Chat —6E 14
Birch Gro. Hem —5A 16
Birch Ho. Barm —1D 34
(off Springwood Rd.)
Birch Ho. Sit —5F 21
Birchington Clo. Maid —6B 30
Bircholt Rd. Maid —1E 42
Birch Tree Way. Maid —1A 36
Birchwood Rd. Maid —6F 29
Birkdale Ct. Maid —7H 29
Birkhall Clo. Chat —4E 14
Birling Av. Bear —7E 30
Birling Av. Rain —7D 10
Birling Clo. Maid —7E 30
Birling Rd. Snod —3B 22
Birling Rd. W Mal —2C 26
Birnam Sq. Maid —7H 29
Bishop Ct. Mil R —4C 20
(off St Paul's St.)
Bishop La. Upc —5K 11
Bishopsbourne Grn. Gill —4B 10
Bishops Clo. Nett —6D 32
Bishop's La. Hunt —6A 40
Bishops Wlk. Roch —3B 8
Bishopsway. Maid —7J 29
Black Cotts. Boxl —5H 25
Blacketts Rd. Tonge —3K 21
Blacklands E Mal —4G 27
(in two parts)
Blacklands Dri. E Mal —3G 27
Blackman Clo. Hoo —1H 5
Blackmanstone Way. Maid —4E 28
Black Rock Gdns. Hem —5B 16
Blacksmith Dri. Weav —6C 30
Blackthorn Av. Chat —6E 14
Blackthorn Dri. Lark —1J 27
Blackthorne Rd. Gill —1H 17
Blake Dri. Lark —6B 22
Blakeney Clo. Bear —7G 31
Blaker Av. Roch —7C 8
Blatchford Clo. E Mal —2G 27
Bleakwood Rd. Chat —4D 14
Blean Rd. Gill —6C 10
Blean Sq. Maid —5B 30
Blendon Rd. Maid —6B 30
Blenheim Av. Chat —6C 8
Blenheim Clo. Bear —1E 36
Blenheim Rd. Sit —7F 21
Blenheim Rd. W Mal —1A 32
Bligh Way. Roch —1E 6
Blind La. Bred —1K 25
Blind La. Det —2K 25

Blockmakers Ct. Chat —6F 9
Bloomsbury Wlk. Maid —7K 29
(off Wyatt St.)
Bloors La. Rain —7D 10
(in two parts)
Bloors Wharf Rd. Gill —4E 10
Blowers Wood Gro. Hem —6B 16
Bluebell Clo. Gill —2K 9
Blue Bell Hill By-Pass. Chat —1A 24
Blue Boar La. Roch —3A 8
Bluett St. Maid —5K 29
Blythe Clo. Sit —4G 21
Blythe Rd. Maid —7A 30
Boarley Ct. S'lng —2J 29
Boarley La. S'lng —2J 29
(in two parts)
Boarley Rd. S'lng —2J 29
Bobbing Hill. Bob —4H 19
Bockingford Ct. Maid —4J 35
Bockingford Ho. Maid —4J 35
Bockingford La. Maid —4J 35
Bockingford Mill Cotts. Maid —4J 35
Bodiam Clo. Gill —5C 10
Bodsham Cres. Bear —2G 37
Boley Hill. Roch —2A 8
Bolner Clo. Chat —7D 14
Bombay Ho. Maid —7D 36
Bondfield Rd. E Mal —3G 27
Bond Rd. Gill —5E 16
Bonflower La. Lin —6F 41
Bonflower La. Lin —6F 41
Bonham Dri. Sit —4E 20
Bonnington Grn. Gill —5C 10
Bonnington Rd. Maid —5B 30
Boormans Cotts. W'bury —5D 32
Bootham Clo. Roch —4F 7
Booth Rd. Chat —6D 8
Borden La. B'den —7K 19
Borough Rd. Gill —4H 9
Borstal M. Roch —6J 7
Borstal Rd. Roch —5J 7
Borstal St. Roch —6J 7
Boston Gdns. Gill —7C 10
Boston Rd. Chat —7G 15
Bottlescrew Hill. Bou M —1A 42
Boughton Clo. Gill —5C 10
Boughton La. Maid —5A 36
Boughton Pde. Maid —5K 35
Boundary Rd. Chat —5B 8
Bounds, The. Ayle —2B 28
Bourncrete Ho. Sit —4E 20
Bourne Gro. Sit —4A 20
Bourneside Ter. Holl —2E 38
Bournewood Clo. Down —3E 36
Bournville Av. Chat —7D 8
Bower Clo. Maid —7H 29
Bower Grn. Chat —1G 25
Bower La. Maid —1H 35
Bower Mt. Rd. Maid —1G 35
Bower Pl. Maid —1H 35
Bower St. Maid —7H 29
Bower Ter. Maid —1H 35
Bowesden La. Shorne —6A 2
Bowes Rd. Roch —7K 3
Bow Hill. W'bury & Yald —6F 33
Bowman Clo. Chat —4G 15
Bow Rd. W'bury —6F 33
Bow Ter. W'bury —5F 33
Boxley Clo. Maid —3A 30
Boxley Grange Cotts. Boxl —5K 25
Boxley Rd. Maid —5K 29
Boxley Rd. W'slde —7E 14
Boxmend Ind. Est. Maid —1E 42
Boyces Hill. N'tn —3E 18
Boyd Bus. Cen. Roch —1B 8
Bracken Ct. Sit —4G 21
Bracken Hill. Chat —1E 24
Bracken Lea. Chat —7G 9
Brackley Clo. Maid —6B 30
Bradbourne Av. Gill —4C 10
Bradbourne La. Dit —2J 27
Bradbourne Pk. Rd. E Mal —2H 27
Braddick Clo. Maid —6A 36
Bradfields Av. Chat —3D 14
Bradfields Av. W. Chat —3D 14
Bradley Dri. Sit —7C 20
Bradley Rd. Up H'lng —4A 12
Braes, The. High —4E 2
Brake Av. Chat —4C 14
Bramble Clo. Maid —1E 34
Brambledown. Chat —1F 15
Brambletree Cotts. Roch —6G 7
Brambletree Cres. Roch —6H 7

Bramley Clo. Gill —1H 17
Bramley Cres. Bear —1E 36
Bramley Gdns. Cox —2G 41
Bramley Rise. Roch —7G 3
Bramley Rd. Snod —2C 22
Bramley Way. King H —2B 32
Bramshott Clo. Maid —5F 29
Bransgore Clo. Gill —2D 16
Brasenose Rd. Gill —5J 9
Brassey Dri. Ayle —3A 28
Brasted Ct. Roch —6J 3
Bray Gdns. Maid —7J 35
Breach La. Lwr Hal —2B 18
Bredgar Clo. Maid —6A 30
Bredgar Rd. Gill —4A 10
Bredhurst Rd. Gill —3B 16
Brenchley Clo. Roch —6B 8
Brenchley Ho. Maid —6J 29
Brenchley Rd. Gill —6B 10
Brenchley Rd. Maid —2J 35
Brenchley Rd. Sit —7D 20
Brendon Av. Chat —6E 14
Brent Clo. Chat —4C 14
Brenzett Clo. Chat —4F 15
Breton Rd. Roch —6A 8
Brett Wlk. Gill —5D 16
Brewers Rd. Shorne —6A 2
Brewer St. Maid —6K 29
Brewery Rd. Sit —3C 20
Briar Clo. Lark —1H 27
Briar Dale. High —3D 2
Briar Fields. Weav —6D 30
Brice Rd. High —4D 2
Brickfields. W Mal —2C 26
Brickfield View. Roch —6A 4
Brickmakers Ind. Est. Sit —3F 21
Bridge Cotts. E Far —4B 34
(St Helens La.)
Bridge Cotts. E Far —5E 34
(Station Hill)
Bridge Hill. Ayle —2B 28
Bridge Ind. Est. Tovil —2H 35
Bridge Mill Way. Tovil —2G 35
Bridge Rd. Gill —1G 9
Bridge Rd. Roch —6A 8
Bridge St. Loose —7J 35
Bridgewater Pl. Leyb —1F 27
Brier Clo. Chat —1G 15
Brier Rd. Sit —4J 19
Bright Rd. Chat —6F 9
Brindle Way. Chat —1G 25
Brisbane Av. Sit —5A 20
Brisbane Rd. Chat —5E 8
Brishing Clo. Maid —7D 36
Brishing La. Bou M —3C 42
Brishing La. Maid —7D 36
Brishing Rd. Maid & Cha S —1D 42
Brisley's Row. Burh —1H 23
Brissenden Clo. Upnor —4E 4
Bristol Clo. Roch —3F 7
Bristol Ho. Maid —5C 36
Britannia Bus. Pk. Quar W —4B 28
Britannia Clo. Hall —5C 12
Britannia Clo. Sit —2C 20
Britton Farm Rd. Gill —2G 9
Britton St. Gill —3F 9
(in two parts)
Broader La. Det —1G 31
Broadfield Rd. Maid —4K 35
Broadlands Dri. Chat —5F 15
Broadoak. Leyb —1E 26
Broadoak Av. Maid —5K 35
Broad St. Sut V —6K 43
Broadview Av. Gill —1E 16
Broadwater Rd. W Mal —6E 26
Broadway. Gill —5A 10
Broadway. Maid —1J 35
Broadway Shop. Cen. Maid —7J 29
Broadwood Rd. Chatt —3E 4
Brockenhurst Av. Maid —3A 36
Brockenhurst Clo. Gill —2C 16
Brogden Cres. Leeds —6A 38
Brogden Farm Cotts. Leeds —5A 38
Bromley Clo. Chat —5F 15
(in two parts)
Bromley Clo. N'tn —4C 18
(in two parts)
Brompton Clo. Chat —2D 8
Brompton Farm Rd. Roch —6H 3
Brompton Hill. Chat —2D 8
Brompton La. Roch —7J 3
Brompton Rd. Gill —2F 9
Bronington Clo. Chat —4E 14

Montfort Rd. Chat —7C **14**
Montfort Rd. Roch —1J **7**
Montgomery Av. Chat —2E **14**
Montgomery Cotts. Up H'lng —4A **12**
Montgomery Rd. Gill —4G **9**
Montpelier Ga. Maid —6E **28**
Moonstone Dri. Chat —7F **15**
Moore St. Roch —7J **3**
Mooring Rd. Roch —7B **8**
Moor Pk. Clo. Gill —1G **17**
Moor St. Rain —1H **17**
Morden Ct. Roch —4A **8**
Morden St. Roch —4A **8**
Morement Rd. Hoo —1H **5**
Morgan Rd. Roch —7J **3**
Morhen Clo. Snod —3A **22**
Morland Dri. Roch —6J **3**
Morris Clo. E Mal —2G **27**
Morris Ct. Clo. Bap —7H **21**
Morse Ho. Sit —6G **21**
Mosquito Rd. W Mal —1A **32**
Mossbank. Chat —6E **14**
Mossy Glade. Gill —3E **16**
Mostyn Rd. Maid —7B **30**
Mote Av. Maid —1A **36**
Mote Rd. Maid —1K **35**
Motney Hill Rd. Gill —5G **11**
Mountbatten Av. Chat —2E **14**
Mountbatten Av. High —3E **2**
Mount Cotts. Bear —7G **31**
Mount Dri. Bear —7G **31**
Mount La. Bear —7G **31**
Mount La. H'lip —6K **17**
Mt. Pleasant. Ayle —7J **23**
Mt. Pleasant. Chat —4F **9**
Mt. Pleasant Dri. Bear —6F **31**
Mount Rd. Chat —5D **8**
Mount Rd. Roch —6J **7**
Mountsfield Clo. Maid —6G **29**
Mount, The. Chat —4D **8**
Mountview. B'den —7K **19**
Moyle Clo. Gill —5D **16**
Mozart Ct. Chat —5C **8**
Muddy La. Sit —7F **21**
Muir Rd. Maid —1K **35**
Mulberry Clo. Hem —5A **16**
Mulberry Ct. Maid —6A **30**
Munn's La. H'lip —3A **18**
Murrain Dri. Down —3F **37**
Murray Rd. Roch —6A **4**
Murston Rd. Sit —6F **21**
Museum Av. Maid —6J **29**
Museum St. Maid —7J **29**
Musgrave Rd. Sit —3D **20**
Musket La. Holl —2B **38** (in two parts)
Mustang Rd. W Mal —1A **32**
Mynn Cres. Bear —7F **31**
Myrtle Cres. Chat —4D **14**

Nagpur Ho. Maid —7D **36**
Nags Head La. Roch —4B **8**
Napier Clo. Sit —5A **20**
Napier Ct. Maid —4J **29**
Napier Rd. Gill —4H **9**
Napwood Clo. Gill —3D **16**
Nares Rd. Gill —5D **16**
Nash Clo. Chat —7G **15**
Nashenden Farm La. Roch —7H **7**
Nashenden La. Roch —6H **7**
Natal Rd. Chat —6E **8**
Nativity Clo. Sit —5C **20**
Naylor's Cotts. Gill —7B **16**
Neale St. Chat —6D **8**
Neath Ct. Maid —4D **36**
Nelson Ct. Chat —7G **9**
Nelson Ho. Maid —7E **36**
Nelson Rd. Gill —4H **9**
Nelson Rd. Woul —5E **12**
Nelson Ter. Chat —7G **9**
Nelson Wlk. Sit —4K **19**
Neptune Bus. Ct. Roch —1C **8**
Neptune Clo. Roch —1C **8**
Neptune Way. Roch —2C **8**
Nestor Ct. Tstn —4H **33**
Netley Clo. Maid —5C **30**
Nettlestead La. Mere —6B **32**
Nevill Ct. W Mal —2D **26**
Neville Clo. Maid —3A **30**
Neville Rd. Chat —6C **8**
Nevill Pl. Snod —3C **22**
Nevill Rd. Snod —3C **22**
Newark Rd. W'sham —3H **21**
Newark Ter. Roch —1K **7**
Newark Yd. Roch —1K **7**
New Barns Rd. Maid —3K **29**
Newbridge Av. Sit —2C **20**
Newbury Av. Maid —4F **29**
Newchurch Rd. Maid —3K **35**
New Convenant Pl. Roch —4B 8 (off New Rd.)
New Covenant Pl. Roch —4B **8**
New Cut. Chat —4D **8**
New Cut. E Far —5G **35**
New Cut Rd. Weav —7C **30**
New Delhi Ho. Maid —7D **36**
Neweden Clo. Maid —5B **30**
Newenden Rd. Wain —5A **4**
New Hythe Bus. Pk. Lark —7D **22**
New Hythe Ho. Lark & Ayle —6D **22**
New Hythe La. Lark & Ayle —2H **27**
Newington Enterprise Cen. N'tn —1E **18**
Newington Ind. Est. H'lip —3B **18**
Newington Wlk. Maid —5B **30**
New Inn Cotts. E Far —5F 35 (off Forge La.)
Newitt Rd. Hoo —2J **5**
Newlands Av. Sit —5K **19**
Newlyn Ct. Maid —7K **29**
Newman Dri. Kem —1D **20**
Newnham Clo. Gill —6C **10**
Newnham St. Chat —5F **9**
New Rd. Burh —1H **23**
New Rd. Chat —4D **8**
New Rd. Dit —2K **27**
New Rd. E Mal —3H **27**
New Rd. Langl —6H **37**
New Rd. Roch —4B **8**
New Rd. Av. Chat —4C **8**
New Rd. Bus. Est. Dit —3J **27**
New Stairs. Chat —2D **8**
New St. Chat —5C **8**
Newton Clo. Chat —7G **15**
Newton Clo. Maid —1H **35**
New Vs. Maid —5F **35**
Nicholas Clo. Barm —1D **34**
Nicklaus Dri. Chat —6D **14**
Nickleby Clo. Roch —6A **8**
Nightingale Clo. Gill —3E **16**
Nightingale Clo. Lark —1G **27**
Nile Rd. Gill —4G **9**
Nine Acres Rd. Cux —5D **6**
Niven Clo. Wain —5A **4**
Norah La. High —3D **2**
Norfolk Clo. Chat —6G **15**
Norfolk Clo. Gill —6D **10**
Norfolk Rd. Maid —4B **36**
Norman Clo. Gill —5B **16**
Norman Clo. Maid —5A **30**
Norman Clo. Roch —4H **7**
Norman Rd. Snod —4C **22**
Norman Rd. W Mal —2B **26**
Norreys Rd. Gill —2E **16**
Norrington Rd. Maid —6K **35**
N. Bank Clo. Roch —3H **7**
Northbank Ho. Roch —2B **8**
Northbourne Rd. Gill —4B **10**
Northcote Rd. Roch —1J **7**
North Ct. Maid —3K **35**
North Cres. Cox —1G **41**
N. Dane Way. Chat —2G **15**
Northdown Clo. Maid —4A **30**
N. Downs Ho. Up H'lng —4A **12**
Northfields. Maid —2C **34**
Northfleet Clo. Maid —6B **30**
N. Folly Rd. E Far —2C **40**
North Ga. Roch —2A **8**
Northleigh Clo. Maid —6K **35**
Northpoint Bus. Est. Roch —7C **4**
N. Pole Rd. E Mal & Barm —2G **33**
North Rd. Cha S —4H **43**
North Rd. Chat —1E **8**
North St. Barm —1B **34**
North St. Sit —2C **20**
North St. Strood —1K **7**
North St. Sut V —6K **43**
North Ter. Chatt —1D **4**
Northumberland Av. Gill —7F **11**
Northumberland Ct. Maid —5C 36 (off Northumberland Rd.)
Northumberland Rd. Maid —5B **36**
North View. Maid —3A **36**
N. View Cotts. Maid —5F **35**
North Way. Maid —4A **30**
Norton Gro. Chat —5C **14**
Norton Rd. Cha S —4H **43**
Norway Ter. Maid —4K **29**
Norwich Clo. Roch —2F **7**
Norwich Ho. Maid —5C **36**
Norwood Wlk. Sit —4K **19**
Norwood Wlk. E. Sit —4A **20**
Norwood Wlk. W. Sit —3K **19**
Nottingham Av. Maid —5C **36**
Nottingham Wlk. Roch —2F **7**
Nursery Av. Bear —1G **37**
Nursery Av. Maid —5E **28**
Nursery Gdns. Hoo —2J **5**
Nursery Rd. Dit —2K **27**
Nursery Rd. Gill —1D **16**
Nutfield Clo. Chat —1F **15**
Nutfields Sit —6F **21**
Nutwood Clo. Weav —7D **30**

Oakapple Ho. Maid —1D **34**
Oakapple La. Barm —1C **34**
Oak Av. Gill —2J **9**
Oak Cotts. Bear —7H 31 (off Green, The)
Oak Cotts. Langl —2A **42**
Oak Dri. High —4D **2**
Oak Dri. Lark —1H **27**
Oakfields. Sit —6A **20**
Oakhurst Clo. Chat —6D **14**
Oakland Clo. Chat —6D **14**
Oak La. Upc —2J **17**
Oakleigh Clo. W'slde —7C **14**
Oak Rd. Roch —2G **7**
Oak Rd. Sit —5G **21**
Oaks Bus. Village, The. Chat —1G **25**
Oaks Dene. Chat —2D **24**
Oaks, The. Ayle —2B **28**
Oak Ter. Chat —7E **14**
Oak Tree Av. Maid —5B **36**
Oaktree Ho. Sit —6F 21 (off Woodberry Dri.)
Oakum Ct. Chat —6F **9**
Oakwood Ct. Maid —1G **35**
Oakwood Rd. Maid —1F **35**
Oast Ct. Sit —7C **20**
Oastview. Rain —1G **17**
Ocelot Ct. Chat —5F **9**
Octavia Ct. Chat —6F **15**
Odiham Dri. Maid —4F **29**
Offham Rd. W Mal —4A **26**
Officer's Rd. Chat —7F **5**
Officers Ter. Chat —2D 8 (off Church La.)
Old Barn Clo. Hem —3K **15**
Old Barn Rd. Leyb —1E **26**
Old Carriage Way, The. Gill —5K **15**
Old Castle Wlk. Gill —5D **16**
Old Chatham Rd. Blue B —3B **24**
Old Chatham Rd. S'lng —5C **24**
Oldchurch Ct. Maid —1H **35**
Old Chu. Rd. Burh —7E **12**
Old Cotts. Maid —2H **35**
Old Dri. Maid —6J **35**
Oldfield Clo. Gill —1D **16**
Oldfield Clo. Maid —3D **36**
Old Ho. La. H'lip —5A **18**
Old Loose Clo. Loose —1J **41**
Old Loose Hill. Loose —1J **41**
Old Manor Cotts. Bear —7H 31 (off Green, The)
Old Mill Cotts. Holl —3A **38**
Old Mill La. Ayle —7A **24**
Old Mill Rd. Holl —4A **38**
Old Oast Bus. Cen., The. Ayle —2D **28**
Old Orchard La. Leyb —2E **26**
Old Orchard, The. Rain —7G **11**
Old Parsonage Ct. W Mal —4D **26**
Old Pattens La. Roch —5B **8**
Old Rd. Chat —4D **8**
Old Rd. W'bury —5C **32**
Old Ryarsh La. W Mal —2C **26**
Old School Clo. Burh —1H **23**
Old School Ct. Chatt —3D **4**
Old Tovil Rd. Maid —2J **35**
Old Trafford Clo. Maid —5E **28**
Old Tree La. Bou M —2B **42**
Old Vinters Rd. Maid —7A **30**
Old Watling St. Roch —7D **2**
Old Well Ct. Maid —2H **35**
Oliver Clo. Chat —6F **9**
Olivers Cotts. Bear —7H **31**
Oliver Twist Clo. Roch —4K **7**
Olivine Clo. Chat —2E **24**
Olliffe Clo. Chat —7D **14**
Onslow Rd. Roch —5B **8**
Opal Grn. Chat —7F **15**
Orache Dri. Weav —6D **30**
Orange Ter. Roch —3B **8**
Orbit Clo. Chat —2E **24**
Orchard Av. Ayle —2B **28**
Orchard Av. Roch —6H **3**
Orchard Bank. Cha S —4G **43**
Orchard Bus. Cen. All —3F **29**
Orchard Clo. Cox —2F **41**
Orchard Clo. Langl —1K **43**
Orchard Clo. Maid —1K **35**
Orchard Cotts. Maid —4D **34**
Orchard Dri. N'tn —4C **18**
Orchard Dri. Weav —1D **36**
Orchard Gro. Dit —1J **27**
Orchard Ind. Est. Maid —2E **42**
Orchard Pl. Maid —1H **35**
Orchard Pl. Sit —6E **20**
Orchard St. Gill —2E **16**
Orchard St. Maid —1K **35**
Orchard, The. Bear —7G **31**
Orchard Vs. Chat —5D **8**
Orchard Way. Snod —3B **22**
Orchid Clo. Roch —2E **6**
Orchid Pk. Roch —5B **8**
Ordnance St. Chat —5C **8**
Ordnance Ter. Chat —4C **8**
Oriel Ho. Roch —3A **8**
Oriole Way. Lark —1G **27**
Orion Rd. Roch —2A **14**
Ormsby Grn. Gill —6E **16**
Orpines, The. W'bury —5G **33**
Orwell Clo. Lark —7B **22**
Orwell Ho. Maid —4D **36**
Orwell Spike. W Mal —6B **26**
Osbourne Dri. Det —1H **31**
Osbourne Rd. Gill —3H **9**
Osprey Ct. Sit —6E **20**
Osprey Wlk. Lark —2G **27**
Ostlers Clo. Snod —2C **22**
Ostlers Ct. High —1E **2**
Otham La. Bear —2H **37**
Otham St. Otham & Bear —5G **37**
Otterbourne Pl. Maid —3D **36**
Otterham Quay La. Rain —1H **17**
Otteridge Rd. Bear —1F **37**
Otway St. Chat —5E **8**
Otway St. Gill —2H **9**
Otway Ter. Chat —5E **8**
Owen Clo. E Mal —3G **27**
Oxford Rd. Gill —5H **9**
Oxford Rd. Maid —4C **36**
Oxford St. Snod —2C **22**
Oxley Shaw La. Leyb —2E **26**
Oyster Clo. Sit —3C **20**

Packer Pl. Chat —1E **14**
Paddock Cotts. Woul —4E **12**
Paddocks, The. Hem —4A **16**
Paddock, The. Chat —4D **8**
Pad's Hill. Maid —7K **29**
Padsole La. Maid —7K **29**
Padstow Mnr. Gill —2G 9 (off Arden St.)
Paget Row. Gill —3G **9**
Paget St. Gill —3F **9**
Pagitt St. Chat —6C **8**
Palace Av. Maid —7K **29**
Palace Ct. Chat —6H **9**
Palace Ind. Est. Maid —1E **42**
Palm Cotts. Maid —1H **41**
Palmer Rd. Maid —5G **29**
Palmerston Rd. Chat —1D **14**
Palmerston Wlk. Sit —5G **21**
Pankhurst Rd. Hoo —1H **5**
Panteny La. Bap —7J **21**
Panton Clo. Chat —5G **15**
Papion Gro. Chat —7C **14**
Papyrus Way. Lark —6D **22**
Parham Rd. Chat —6D **8**
Park Av. Gill —6H **9**
Park Av. Lin —3H **41**
Park Av. Maid —5A **30**
Park Av. Sit —7C **20**
Park Barn Rd. Broom —7C **38**
Park Cres. Chat —1D **14**
Parker Clo. Gill —4E **16**
Park Farm. Dit —3J **27**
Parkfield Rd. Gill —6F **11**
Parkfields. Roch —1E **6**
Park Ho. Maid —5A **30**
Park La. Bou M —3C **42**
Park La. Maid —4J **29**
Park Mnr. Gill —3G **9**
Park Pale. Roch —7B **2**
Park Rd. Mere —7A **32**
Park Rd. Sit —7C **20**
Park View Clo. Maid —3D **36**
Park Way. Cox —2F **41**
Park Way. Maid —3A **36**
Park Wood Grn. Shop. Cen. Gill —4D **16**
Park Wood Pde. Maid —7E **36**
Park Wood Trad. Est. Maid —1F **43**
Parr Av. Gill —2H **9**
Parrs Head M. Roch —2A **8**
Parsonage Ct. W Mal —3D **26**
Parsonage La. Bob —1H **19**
Parsonage La. Roch —6A **4**
Partridge Av. Lark —7B **22**
Pasley Rd. Gill —2E **8**
Pasley Rd. E. Chat —1F **9**
Pasley Rd. N. Chat —1F **9**
Pasley Rd. W. Chat —1E **8**
Patrixbourne Av. Gill —6C **10**
Pattens Gdns. Roch —6B **8**
Pattens La. Chat —6B **8**
Pattens Pl. Roch —6B **8**
Pavilion Dri. Kem —1D **20**
Pavilion La. Mere —4B **32**
Pavings, The. Holl —2D **38**
Payne's La. Maid —5K **35**
Peace Cotts. Maid —6A **40**
Peacock M. Maid —7H **29**
Peal Clo. Hoo —2J **5**
Pearman Clo. Gill —7G **11**
Pear Tree All. Sit —4C 20 (off St Paul's St.)
Pear Tree Av. Dit —2K **27**
Pear Tree La. Hem —1J **15**
Pear Tree La. Maid —6A **36**
Peartree La. Shorne —6A **2**
Peartree Pl. High —4D **2**
Pear Tree Row. Langl —7G **37**
Pear Tree Wlk. N'tn —4C **18**
Peckham Clo. Roch —7A **4**
Peel Dri. Sit —5G **21**
Peel St. Maid —5K **29**
Peel St. Hedges. Maid —4K **29**
Peens La. Bou M —5B **42**
Peggoty Clo. High —4D **2**
Pelican Clo. Roch —2E **6**
Pelican Ct. W'bury —5F **33**
Pemberton Sq. Roch —7A **4**
Pembroke. Chat —7E **4**
Pembroke Gdns. Gill —5E **16**
Pembroke Rd. Cox —2E **40**
Pembury Ct. Sit —5C 20 (off Pembury St.)
Pembury Gdns. Maid —1G **35**
Pembury St. Sit —5C **20**
Pembury Way. Gill —6E **10**
Penenden Ct. Maid —4A **30**
Penenden Heath Rd. Maid —4B **30**
Penenden St. Maid —5K **29**
Penfold Clo. Chat —2F **15**
Penfold Clo. Maid —7D **36**
Penfold Hill. Leeds —4C **38**
Penfold Way. Maid —6J **35**
Penguin Clo. Roch —2F **7**
Penhurst Clo. Weav —6E **30**
Pennant Rd. Roch —2A **14**
Penn Clo. Sit —7F **21**
Pennine Way. Down —3F **37**
Penryn Mnr. Gill —2G 9 (off Skinner St.)
Penshurst Clo. Gill —6E **10**
Penstocks, The. Maid —2G **35**
Pentagon Cen. Chat —4D **8**
Pepper All. Maid —3H **29**
Pepy's Way. Roch —1H **7**
Peregrine Dri. Sit —6E **20**
Peregrine Rd. King H —2B **32**
Perie Row. Gill —2E 8 (off Middle St.)
Perimeter Rd. Lark —7E **22**
Periwinkle Clo. Sit —4C **20**
Perryfield St. Maid —5J **29**
Perry St. Chat —5C **8**
Perry St. Maid —5J **29**
Perth Gdns. Sit —5A **20**
Pested Bars Rd. Bou M —7B **36**
Peterborough Gdns. Roch —2E **6**
Peters Works. Woul —6E **12**
Petham Grn. Gill —5C **10**
Peverel Dri. Bear —7E **30**
Peverel Grn. Gill —5D **16**
Pheasant La. Maid —5A **36**
Pheasant Rd. Chat —6G **9**
Phillippa Ct. Mil R —2C **20**
Phillips Ct. Gill —6B **10**
Phoenix Cotts. W'bury —6E 32 (off Maidstone Rd.)

Phoenix Dri. W'bury —5F 33
Phoenix Ind. Est. Strood —1B 8
Phoenix Pk. Bus. Cen. Maid —1E 42
Phoenix Rd. Chat —7F 15
Phoenix Wharf. Roch —1B 8
Pickering St. Maid —7K 35
Pickwick Cres. Roch —6A 8
Pier App. Rd. Gill —1H 9
Pier Pl. Roch —4E 4
Pier Rd. Gill —1H 9
Pier Rd. Ind. Est. Gill —1H 9
Pikefields. Gill —6C 10
Pikey La. E Mal —6E 26
Pilgrim Cotts. Up H'lng —4A 12
Pilgrims View. S'lng —7C 24
Pilgrims View. Snod —2B 22
Pilgrims Way. Boxl & Holl —6F 25
Pilgrims Way. Burh —3J 23
Pilgrims Way. Cux —5E 6
Pilgrims Way. Up H'lng —6A 12
Pilot Rd. Roch —1A 14
Pimpernal Clo. Bear —7G 31
Pimpernel Way. Chat —5C 14
Pimps Ct. Cotts. Maid —6H 35
Pine Clo. Lark —1H 27
Pine Cotts. All —3H 29
Pine Gro. Hem —3A 16
Pine Gro. Maid —5A 30
Pine Ho. Chat —4D 14
Pine Lodge. Maid —1F 35
Pine Lodge Cvn. Pk. Holl —2A 38
Pine Pl. Tovil —3H 35
Pine Rd. Roch —2H 7
Pinewood Dri. Chat —2H 25
Pintails, The. St Mi —6F 5
Piper's Cotts. Maid —1H 41
Pippin Clo. Cox —3E 40
Pippin Clo. Sit —3B 20
Pippin Way. King H —2B 32
Pippon Croft. Hem —3A 16
Pirbright Clo. Chat —7H 15
Pitt Rd. Kgswd —2K 43
Pitt Rd. Maid —3E 34
Pizien Well Rd. W'bury —6B 32
Place La. H'lip —4K 17
Plains Av. Maid —3A 36
Plaistow Sq. Maid —5B 30
Plantation La. Bear —7F 31
Plantation Rd. Gill —2A 10
Platters Farm Lodge. Gill —2D 16
Platters, The. Gill —1C 16
Platt, The. Sut V —6K 43
Playstool Clo. N'tn —3D 18
Playstool Rd. N'tn —3C 18
Pleasant Courts. Det —2F 31
Pleasant Row. Chat —2E 8
Pleasant Row. Roch —3A 8
Pleasant Valley La. Maid —1E 40
Plomley Clo. Gill —5D 16
Plough Cotts. Langl —3J 43
Ploughmans Way. Chat —1E 24
Ploughmans Way. Gill —3E 16
Plough Wents Rd. Cha S —3E 42
Plover Clo. Chat —1H 25
Plover Rd. Lark —1G 27
Pluckley Clo. Gill —5C 10
Plumpton Wlk. Maid —6E 36
Plumtree Gro. Hem —5A 16
Plumtrees. Maid —2D 34
Poachers Clo. Chat —4G 15
Pochard Clo. St Mi —6F 5
Podkin Wood. Chat —2D 24
Polhill Dri. Chat —7D 14
Police Sta. Rd. W Mal —3D 26
Pond Dri. Sit —7E 20
Pondfield La. Shorne —6A 2
Pope St. Maid —2F 35
Poplar Clo. Roch —3H 7
Poplar Gro. Maid —6E 28
Poplar Rd. Roch —3G 7
Poplicans Rd. Cux —5D 6
Poppy Clo. Gill —3J 9
Poppy Clo. Maid —1G 35
Porchester Clo. Maid —6K 35
Port Clo. Chat —6F 15
Porters Wlk. Langl —1K 43
Portland Av. Sit —5G 21
Portland Pl. Snod —2C 22
Portland Rd. Gill —2J 9
Portland Rd. Woul —5E 12
Portland St. Chat —6F 9
Port Rise. Chat —5D 8
Portsdown Clo. Maid —2E 34
Portsmouth Clo. Roch —2F 7
Post Barn Rd. Chat —6D 8
Postley Commercial Cen. Maid —2K 35
Postley Ind. Cen. Maid —3K 35
Postley Rd. Maid —3K 35
Postmill Dri. Maid —3J 35
Pottery Rd. Hoo —2H 5
Potyn Ho. Roch —4A 8
Poulsen Ct. Sit —6F 21
Pout Rd. Snod —3B 22
Povey Av. Wain —5A 4
Powell Clo. Ayle —7J 23
Powlett Rd. Roch —6A 4
Pratling St. Ayle —7K 23
Precinct, The. Roch —3A 8
Premier Pde. Ayle —2B 28
Prentis Clo. Sit —4A 20
Prentis Quay. Sit —4C 20
Preston Av. Gill —7J 9
Preston Way. Gill —6C 10
Pretoria Ho. Maid —7D 36
Pretoria Rd. Chat —6D 8
Pretoria Rd. Gill —5H 9
Pridmore Rd. Snod —2B 22
Priestfield Rd. Gill —3J 9
Priestfields. Roch —5K 7
Priestley Dri. Lark —6B 22
Primrose Av. Gill —4B 16
Primrose Clo. Chat —2C 14
Primrose Cotts. Maid —4G 37
Primrose Dri. Dit —2A 28
Primrose Rd. Up H'lng —4A 12
Prince Arthur Rd. Gill —2F 9
Prince Charles Av. Chat —5F 15
Prince Charles Av. Sit —7F 21
Princes Av. Chat —6E 14
Princess Mary Av. Chat —1F 9
Princes St. Maid —6K 29
Prince's St. Roch —4A 8
Princes Way. Det —2F 31
Prinys Dri. Gill —5C 16
Priors Dean Clo. Barm —3B 34
Priors Ga. Roch —3A 8
Priory Clo. E Far —4E 34
Priory Ct. Gill —6A 10
Priory Ga. Maid —6K 29
Priory Gro. Dit —2A 28
Priory Rd. Gill —6A 10
Priory Rd. Maid —1K 35
Priory Rd. Roch —2J 7
Priory, The. E Far —4F 35
Progress Est., The. Maid —7F 37
Prospect Av. Roch —7K 3
Prospect Pl. Maid —1H 35
Prospect Pl. Roch —6J 7
Prospect Row. Chat —5E 8
Prospect Row. Gill —2E 8
Provender Way. Weav —6D 30
Providence Cotts. High —5D 2
Providence Pl. Woul —5E 12
Pudding La. Maid —7J 29
Pudding Rd. Rain —1F 17
Pump Clo. Leyb —2E 26
Pump La. Gill —7C 10
(in two parts)
Purbeck Rd. Chat —6C 8
Purser Way. Gill —1G 9
Puttney Dri. Kem —1E 20
Pyrus Clo. Chat —2F 25

Quarries, The. Bou M —1B 42
Quarry Cotts. Langl —1A 42
Quarry Rd. Maid —2K 35
Quarry Sq. Maid —6K 29
Quarry Wood Ind. Est. Ayle —3B 28
Quayside. Chat —7F 5
Queen Anne Rd. Maid —7K 29
Queen Ct. Roch —4A 8
Queendown Av. Gill —4D 16
Queen Elizabeth Sq. Maid —6C 36
Queen Mother Ct., The. Roch —4K 7
Queen's Av. Maid —6G 29
Queen's Av. Snod —2C 22
Queen's Farm Rd. Shorne —1A 2
Queens Ho. Maid —1E 34
Queens Rd. Chat —6H 9
Queens Rd. Gill —4G 9
Queen's Rd. Maid —1E 34
Queen's Rd. Snod —2C 22
Queen St. Chat —4E 8
Queen St. Roch —4A 8
(in two parts)
Queensway. Det —2F 31
Queenswood Rd. Ayle —3B 24
Quern, The. Maid —3H 35
Quested Way. H'shm —6K 39
Quickthorn Cres. Chat —4C 14
Quinell St. Gill —7E 10
Quinion Clo. Chat —2D 24
Quinton Rd. Mil R —2A 20
Quixote Cres. Roch —6K 3

Racefield Clo. Shorne —6A 2
Radleigh Gdns. Chat —7C 8
Raggatt Pl. Maid —2A 36
Ragstone Ct. Dit —3K 27
Ragstone Rd. Bear —2F 37
Railway St. Chat —4C 8
Railway St. Gill —3H 9
Railway St. Ind. Est. Gill —2H 9
Rainham Clo. Maid —3J 35
Rainham Shop. Cen. Rain —7F 11
Raleigh Clo. Chat —3E 14
Ramillies Clo. Chat —4E 14
Rampion Clo. Weav —6D 30
Randall Rd. Chat —7C 8
Randalls Row. Loose —7J 35
Randall St. Maid —5J 29
Randolph Cotts. Roch —6K 3
Randolph Ho. Gill —3G 9
Randolph Rd. Gill —3G 9
Ranscombe Clo. Roch —3F 7
Ratcliffe Highway. Chatt —2E 4
Raven Clo. Lark —2H 27
Ravens Dane Clo. Down —3F 37
Ravenswood Av. Roch —7K 3
Rawdon Rd. Maid —1K 35
Raymer Rd. Maid —3A 30
Reading Ho. Maid —7E 36
Readscroft Rd. Gill —4D 16
Recreation Av. Snod —2C 22
Recreation Clo. Maid —5A 30
Rectory Clo. Snod —2C 22
Rectory Clo. Woul —4E 12
Rectory Grange. Roch —6A 8
Rectory La. Barm —3C 34
Rectory La. Cha S —7H 43
Rectory La. Sut V —6K 43
Rectory La. N. Leyb —1F 27
Rectory La. S. Leyb —1F 27
Rectory Rd. Sit —7F 21
Reculver Wlk. Maid —5E 36
Redbank. Leyb —1F 27
Redbridge Clo. Chat —4G 15
Redcliffe La. Maid —4K 29
Red Cotts. Maid —3H 29
Rede Ct. Rd. Strood —7F 3
Rede Wood Rd. Maid —1B 34
Redfern Av. Gill —3J 9
Red Hill. W'bury —4F 33
Red Ho. Gdns. W'bury —5D 32
Redland Shaw. Roch —7C 8
Redruth Mnr. Gill —2G 9
(off Cross St.)
Redsells Clo. Down —3F 37
Redvers Rd. Chat —6E 8
Redwall Bungalows. Lin —7G 41
Redwall La. Hunt —6D 40
Redwall La. Lin —6H 41
Redwing Clo. Lark —7B 22
Redwing Rd. Chat —3F 15
Redwood Clo. Chat —7F 15
Reeds Ct. Maid —2G 35
Reform Rd. Chat —6F 9
Regency Clo. Gill —6C 16
Regency Ct. Sit —5B 20
Regent Dri. Maid —4K 35
Regent Rd. Gill —4G 9
Reginald Av. Cux —5E 6
Reginald Rd. Maid —1H 35
Regis Cres. Sit —3C 20
Reinden Gro. Down —3E 36
Renown Rd. Chat —7G 15
Repton Way. Chat —5D 14
Reservoir Cotts. Up H'lng —5A 12
Resolution Clo. Chat —4E 14
Restharrow Rd. Weav —7D 30
Retreat Cvn. Pk., The. Nett —6E 32
Revenge Rd. Chat —1G 25
Reynolds Fields. High —1E 2
Rhode Ct. Sit —4A 20
Rhode St. Chat —4E 8
Rhodewood Clo. Down —3F 37
Richard St. Chat —4D 8
Richard St. Roch —5A 8
Richborough Dri. Strood —6J 3
Richmond Clo. Chat —5F 15
Richmond Clo. Upnor —6D 4
Richmond Dri. Sit —2C 20
Richmond Pde. Roch —5B 8
Richmond Rd. Gill —2G 9
Richmond Way. Maid —4K 35
Riddles Rd. Sit —6A 20
Ridgeway Bungalows. Shorne —6B 2
Ridgeway, The. Chat —2C 14
Ridgeway, The. Gill —2G 9
Ridgeway, The. Shorne —6A 2
Ridgway. Maid —2E 34
Ridley Rd. Roch —4K 7
Rigden's Ct. Sit —4C 20
Ringlestone Cres. Maid —3J 29
Ringwood Clo. Gill —1D 16
Ringwood Rd. Maid —4B 36
Ripon Av. Gill —7A 10
Ripon Clo. Gill —5D 10
Ripton Cotts. Tstn —5H 33
Rise, The. B'den —7K 19
Rise, The. Hem —6A 16
Rise, The. Roch —5B 8
Ritch Rd. Snod —2A 22
River Clo. E Far —5E 34
River Dri. Roch —1G 7
Riverhead Clo. Maid —5G 29
Riverhead Clo. Sit —6A 20
Rivers Clo. W'bury —5F 33
Riverside Cvn. Pk. E Far —4D 34
Riverside Est. Roch —2C 8
Riverside View. Ayle —1E 28
River St. Gill —2E 8
River View. Gill —5D 10
River View. Maid —2J 35
River Way. Lark —6C 22
Roach St. Roch —1J 7
Roan Ct. Roch —7H 3
Roberts Clo. Sit —2B 20
Roberts Orchard Rd. Maid —1C 34
Roberts Rd. Gill —1E 16
Roberts Rd. Snod —2B 22
Robin Hood La. W'slde —7D 14
Robin Hood La. Lwr. W'slde —7C 14
Robin Hood La. Up. Blue B —1B 24
Robson Dri. Ayle —1A 28
Robson Dri. Hoo —2H 5
Rocfort Rd. Snod —2C 22
Rochester Av. Roch —4A 8
Rochester Ct. Roch —7C 4
Rochester Cres. Hoo —1H 5
Rochester Ga. Roch —3B 8
Rochester Ho. Maid —5C 36
Rochester Rd. Ayle —7J 23
Rochester Rd. Burh —6F 13
Rochester Rd. Cux —7D 6
(in two parts)
Rochester Rd. Roch & Chat —3A 14
Rochester Rd. Woul —4E 12
Rochester St. Chat —6C 8
Rock Av. Gill —4G 9
Rock Rd. Maid —4K 29
Rock Rd. Sit —6C 20
Rocks Clo. E Mal —5H 27
Rocks Rd., The. E Mal —5H 27
Rocky Hill. Maid —7H 29
Rocky Hill Ter. Maid —7H 29
Roebuck Rd. Roch —3A 8
Roffen Rd. Roch —6A 8
Rolvenden Av. Gill —5C 10
Rolvenden Dri. Sit —4K 19
Rolvenden Rd. Wain —5A 4
Roman Clo. Blue B —1B 24
Roman Heights. Maid —5B 30
Roman Rd. Snod —2B 22
Roman Sq. Sit —6D 20
Roman Way. Roch —4H 7
Romany Ct. Chat —6H 9
Romany Rd. Gill —6B 10
Rome Ter. Chat —4D 8
Romney Clo. Bear —1F 37
Romney Ct. Sit —4B 20
Romney Pl. Maid —7K 29
Romney Rd. Chat —4F 15
Romsey Clo. Roch —7G 3
Ronalds Ct. Sit —5E 20
Rook La. Bob —4G 19
Roonagh Ct. Sit —7C 20
Roosevelt Av. Chat —2D 14
Ropemakers Ct. Chat —7E 8
Roper Clo. Gill —6C 16
Rope Wlk. Chat —3D 8
Roseacre Gdns. Bear —7F 31
Roseacre La. Bear —1F 37
Rosebery Clo. Sit —5H 21
Rosebery Rd. Chat —6C 8
Rosebery Rd. Gill —1H 9
Rose Cotts. Loose —7J 35
(off Old Loose Hill)
Rose Cotts. Roch —7D 2
Roseholme. Maid —2G 35
Roseleigh Av. Maid —7F 29
Roseleigh Rd. Sit —7B 20
Rosemary Clo. Chat —5D 14
Rosemary Rd. Bear —1F 37
Rosemary Rd. E Mal —2G 27
Rosemount Clo. Loose —1J 41
Rosemount Ct. Roch —6J 3
Rose St. Roch —5B 8
Rose Yd. Maid —7K 29
Rosslyn Grn. Maid —6E 28
Ross St. Roch —4B 8
Rother Ho. Maid —4C 36
Rother Vale. Chat —6G 15
Roundel, The. Sit —7D 20
Roundhay. Leyb —2E 26
Roundwell. Bear —7J 31
Rover Rd. Chat —7F 15
Rowan Ho. Maid —1D 34
Rowan Lea. Chat —1F 15
Rowan Wlk. Chat —5C 8
Rowbrocke Clo. Gill —6D 16
Rowe Pl. Eccl —4H 23
Rowland Av. Gill —6J 9
Rowland Clo. Maid —1H 35
Royal Eagle Clo. Roch —1C 8
Royal Engineers Rd. S'lng —2H 29
Royal Sovereign Av. Chat —1F 9
Royal Star Arc. Maid —7J 29
Roydon Hall Rd. E Peck —7A 32
Royston Rd. Bear —1F 37
Roystons Clo. Gill —6F 11
Ruckinge Way. Gill —5C 10
Rudge Clo. Chat —7H 15
Rugby Clo. Chat —5D 14
Rumwood Ct. Langl —7H 37
Running Horse Roundabout. S'lng —2H 29
Runnymede Gdns. Maid —4K 35
Rush Clo. Chat —6E 14
Rushdean Rd. Roch —3F 7
Rushmead Dri. Maid —5K 35
Ruskin Clo. E Mal —3G 27
Russell Clo. Sit —6A 20
Russell Ct. Chat —5F 9
Russell Rd. Ayle —3B 24
Russell's Av. Gill —1G 17
Russet Clo. Roch —7G 3
Russet Ct. Cox —2F 41
Russets, The. Maid —6E 28
Russett Clo. Ayle —3B 28
Russet Way. King H —2A 32
Ruth Ho. Maid —6H 29
Rutland Cotts. Leeds —7K 37
Rutland Pl. Gill —6C 16
Rutland Way. Maid —4D 36
Ryarsh La. W Mal —2C 26
Rycault Clo. Maid —1H 35
Rycaut Clo. Gill —6D 16
Rydal Ho. Maid —5C 36
Ryde Clo. Chat —1F 15
Ryegrass Clo. Chat —3G 15

Sabre Ct. Gill B —7A 10
Saddlers Clo. Weav —6D 30
Sadlers Clo. Chat —7B 14
Saffron Way. Chat —4D 14
Saffron Way. Sit —2D 20
Sail Field Ct. Chat —1D 8
Sailmakers Ct. Chat —6F 9
St Albans Clo. Gill —1J 9
St Alban's Rd. Roch —2F 7
St Alban Wlk. Chat —5C 8
St Andrew's Clo. Barm —2D 34
St Andrews Ho. Maid —1D 34
St Andrews Rd. Gill —1H 9
St Andrew's Rd. Maid —2D 34
St Anne Ct. Maid —7H 29
St Asaph Ho. Maid —5C 36
St Barnabas Clo. All —3F 29
St Barnabas Clo. Gill —5H 9
St Bartholomews La. Roch —4C 8
St Bartholomews Ter. Roch —4C 8
St Benedict Rd. Snod —3A 22
St Catherines Hospital. Roch —4B 8
St Clements Ho. Roch —3B 8
St Edmunds Way. Gill —7G 11

St Faith's La. Bear —7G 31
St Faith's St. Maid —7J 29
St George's Rd. Gill —2G 9
St George's Sq. Maid —1G 35
St Helen's Cotts. Maid —4B 34
St Helens La. E Far —4B 34
St Helier's Clo. Maid —2E 34
St James Clo. E Mal —3G 27
St John's Av. Sit —6F 21
St John's Clo. High —3E 2
St John's Rd. Gill —5G 9
St John's Rd. High —3E 2
St Johns Rd. Hoo —1H 5
St Johns Way. Roch —6J 7
(in two parts)
St Katherine's La. Snod —3B 22
St Laurence Av. Maid —3E 28
St Lawrence Clo. Bap —7H 21
St Leonards Av. Chat —6D 8
St Leonards Rd. All —3F 29
St Leonard's St. W Mal —5B 26
St Lukes Av. Maid —6A 30
St Lukes Rd. Maid —6A 30
St Margarets Bank. Roch —4B 8
St Margarets Banks. Roch —3B 8
St Margaret's Clo. Maid —2E 34
St Margarets Dri. Gill —4C 16
St Margaret's M. Roch —3A 8
St Margaret's St. Roch —4K 7
St Mark's Clo. N'tn —2E 18
St Marks Ct. Eccl —4H 23
St Mark's Ho. Gill —3G 9
St Martin's Clo. Det —2F 31
St Martin's Clo. N'tn —2E 18
St Mary's Ct. W Mal —3C 26
St Mary's Gdns. Chat —1F 9
St Mary's Rd. Gill —2G 9
St Mary's Rd. Roch —1K 7
St Mary's View. N'tn —2E 18
St Mary's Wlk. Burh —1H 23
St Matthew's Clo. N'tn —2E 18
St Matthews Dri. Roch —6J 7
St Michael's Clo. Ayle —7A 24
St Michaels Clo. Chat —5D 8
St Michaels Clo. Sit —5D 20
St Michaels Ct. Strood —7K 3
St Michael's Rd. Maid —1G 35
St Michael's Rd. Sit —5C 20
(in two parts)
St Nicholas Gdns. Roch —1H 7
St Paul's Clo. Roch —3F 7
St Paul's St. Sit —4C 20
(in two parts)
St Peter's Bri. Maid —7J 29
St Peter's Clo. Dit —2J 27
St Peter's Ct. Dit —2J 27
St Peter's Path. Roch —3A 8
St Peter's Pl. Eccl —4H 23
St Peter's Rd. Dit —2J 27
St Peter St. Maid —6J 29
St Peter St. Roch —4B 8
St Philip's Av. Maid —1A 36
St Saviours Rd. Maid —6C 36
St Stephen's Clo. N'tn —2E 18
St Stephen's Cotts. Maid —6B 34
St Stephens M. Roch —1C 14
St Stephen's Sq. Maid —2H 35
St Werburgh Ct. Hoo —2H 5
St Werburgh Cres. Hoo —2H 5
St Werburgh Ter. Hoo —2J 5
St William's Way. Roch —5B 8
Salem St. Maid —1K 35
Salisbury Av. Gill —1D 16
Salisbury Clo. Sit —5G 21
Salisbury Ho. Maid —5C 36
Salisbury Rd. Blue B —2B 24
Salisbury Rd. Chat —5E 8
Salisbury Rd. Maid —5K 29
Sally Port. Gill —2E 8
Sally Port Gdns. Gill —2E 8
Saltings Rd. Snod —3C 22
Salts Av. Loose —2J 41
Salts Farm Cotts. Maid —1K 41
Salts La. Loose —7K 35
Saltwood Rd. Maid —3J 35
Samara Clo. Chat —1E 24
Samphire Clo. Weav —7D 30
Sanctuary Rd. Gill —5A 10
Sandbourne Dri. Maid —2J 29
Sandford Rd. Sit —4K 19
Sandgate Ct. Gill —5F 17
Sandhill La. High —1F 3
Sandhurst Clo. Gill —5C 10
Sandling Ct. Maid —4A 30
Sandling La. S'lng —1H 29
(in two parts)
Sandling Rd. Maid —4J 29
(in two parts)
Sandling Way. St Mi —6F 5
Sandown Dri. Gill —2D 16
Sandown Rd. W Mal —3C 26
Sandpiper Rd. Chat —7H 15
Sandringham Rd. Gill —5E 16
Sandstone Rise. Chat —2G 25
Sandycroft Rd. Roch —6H 3
Sandy Dell. Hem —6A 16
Sandy La. Bear —6G 31
Sandy La. Boxl —2B 30
Sandy La. Snod —4A 22
Sandy La. W Mal —2B 26
Sandy Mt. Bear —6G 31
Sappers Wlk. Gill —3G 9
Saracen Clo. Gill B —7A 10
Saracen Fields. W'slde —2G 25
Sarsen Heights. Chat —1D 24
Sassoon Clo. Lark —6C 22
Satis Av. Sit —2C 20
Saunders St. Chat —5D 8
Saunders St. Gill —2G 9
Savage Rd. Chat —6F 15
Sawyers Ct. Chat —6F 9
Saxon Clo. King H —2A 32
Saxon Clo. Roch —6H 3
Saxon Pl. Roch —3H 7
Saxons Dri. Maid —4A 30
Saxon Shore Way. Gill —1A 10
Saxton St. Gill —3G 9
Scarborough La. Burh —1E 22
Scarlett Clo. Chat —4G 15
Scholars Rise. Roch —1F 7
Scholey Clo. Hall —5D 12
School Av. Gill —4J 9
School La. Bap —6H 21
School La. B'den —5H 19
School La. High —4E 2
School La. Maid —3D 36
School La. N'tn —2D 18
School La. Sut V —6K 43
School Rd. Sit —6F 21
School Rd. Woul —4E 12
School Vs. Nett —7E 32
Schreiber M. Gill —3H 9
Scimitar Clo. Gill B —7A 10
Scotby Av. Chat —5F 15
Scott Av. Gill —1G 17
Scott Clo. Dit —3K 27
Scotteswood Av. Chat —6D 8
Scott's Ter. Chat —5D 8
Scott St. Maid —5J 29
Scraces Cotts. Maid —4D 34
Scragged Oak Cvn. Pk. Det —1G 31
Scragged Oak Rd. Det —1G 31
Scrubbs La. Maid —7G 29
Seaford Ct. Roch —4K 7
Seagull Rd. Roch —2E 6
Sealand Ct. Roch —4K 7
Seamew Ct. Roch —1E 6
Seaton Rd. Gill —5J 9
Seaview Rd. Gill —4G 9
Second Av. Chat —7F 9
Second Av. Gill —5J 9
Secretan Rd. Roch —7K 7
Sedge Cres. Chat —5C 14
Sedley Clo. Ayle —1C 28
Sedley Clo. Gill —6C 16
Sefton Rd. Chat —3G 15
Selbourne Rd. Gill —1H 9
Selbourne Wlk. Maid —6E 36
Selby Rd. Maid —1E 42
Sellinge Grn. Gill —5C 10
Selstead Clo. Gill —7C 10
Semple Gdns. Chat —5C 8
Senacre La. Maid —6D 36
Senacres Cotts. Maid —6E 36
Senacre Sq. Maid —5E 36
Sessions Ho. Sq. Maid —6J 29
Settington Av. Chat —7G 9
Severn Rd. Chat —4G 15
Sevington Pk. Maid —6J 35
Sextant Pk. Roch —2C 8
Seymour Rd. Chat —5F 9
Seymour Rd. Rain —1J 17
Seymour's Cotts. Leeds —6K 37
Shackleton Clo. Chat —3F 15
Shades, The. Roch —1D 6
Shaftesbury Clo. E Mal —2G 27
Shaftesbury Dri. Maid —7F 29
Shakespeare Rd. Gill —4G 9
Shakespeare Rd. Sit —5E 20
Shamel Bus. Cen. Roch —1A 8
Shamley Rd. Chat —7H 15
Shanklin Clo. Chat —1G 15
Sharfleet Dri. Roch —1D 6
Sharnal La. Snod —3C 22
Sharon Cres. Chat —5D 14
Sharsted Way. Bear —6G 31
Sharsted Way. Hem —6A 16
Shawstead Rd. Gill —2G 15
Shaws Way. Roch —5A 8
Shaws Wood. Roch —6K 3
Sheal's Ct. Maid —2K 35
Sheal's Cres. Maid —2K 35
Shearers Clo. Weav —7D 30
Shearwater. Maid —6E 28
Shearwater Clo. Roch —1E 6
Sheldon Dri. Gill —1F 17
(in two parts)
Sheldon Way. Lark —7C 22
Shelley Rd. Maid —2F 35
Shenley Gro. S'lng —1J 29
Shepherds Ga. Hem —4K 15
Shepherds Ga. Dri. Weav —6D 30
Shepherds Way. Langl —1K 43
Shepperton Clo. Chat —5G 15
Sheppey Rd. Maid —5J 35
Sheppey Way. Bob —4J 19
Shepway Ct. Maid —4B 36
Sheraton Ct. Chat —1D 24
Sherbourne Dri. Maid —2E 34
Sherbourne Dri. Strood —6J 3
Sheridan Clo. Chat —2G 15
Sheridan Clo. Maid —3H 29
Sheridan Ct. Roch —6J 7
Sheriff Dri. Chat —7E 14
Sherman Clo. Gill —7B 10
Shernolds. Maid —5A 36
Sherwood Av. Chat —7E 14
Sherwood Ho. Chat —6D 14
Shillingheld Clo. Bear —6E 30
Shingle Barn La. W Far —2A 40
Ship La. Roch —4C 8
Shipley Ct. Maid —7K 29
Shipwrights Av. Chat —7E 8
Shirley Av. Chat —4B 14
Shirley Ct. Maid —7D 36
Shirley Way. Bear —1F 37
Sholden Rd. Roch —6A 4
Shorefields. Rain —6G 11
Shoreham Wlk. Maid —5E 36
Shorland Ct. Roch —4K 7
Shortlands Grn. Maid —7E 36
Shortlands Rd. Sit —5E 20
Short La. Gill —2A 10
Short St. Chat —5F 9
Shorts Way. Roch —5J 7
Shottenden Rd. Gill —1H 9
Shropshire Ter. Maid —5D 36
Shrubsole Dri. S'lng —7D 24
Shurland Av. Sit —7D 20
Sidney Rd. Gill —1G 9
Sidney Rd. Roch —6J 7
Sidney St. Maid —2F 35
Signal Ct. Gill —7F 11
Silchester Ct. Maid —4B 30
Silverbank. Chat —3E 14
Silver Birches. Chat —6E 14
Silverdale. Maid —2C 34
Silverdale Dri. Gill —2F 17
Silverdale Gro. Sit —6A 20
Silver Hill. Chat —5D 8
Silver Hill. Roch —6H 7
Silver Hill Gdns. Chat —5D 8
Silverspot Clo. Rain —2F 17
Silver Tree Clo. Chat —1E 24
Silverweed Rd. Chat —5C 14
Simmonds La. Otham —6G 37
Simpson Rd. Sit —4A 20
Simpson Rd. Snod —4C 22
Sinclair Clo. Gill —5E 16
Sindal Shaw Ho. Chat —5C 14
Sindals La. Chat —1J 25
Singapore Dri. Gill —3E 8
Sir Evelyn Rd. Roch —7K 7
Sir Hawkins Way. Chat —4D 8
Sir Thomas Longley Rd. Roch —2C 8
Siskin Wlk. Lark —1G 27
Sissinghurst Dri. Maid —7E 28
Sittingbourne Ind. Est. Sit —4D 20
Sittingbourne Rd. Det & S'bry —1J 31
Sittingbourne Rd. Maid —6A 30
(in two parts)
Skene Clo. Gill —7G 11
Skinners Clo. Eccl —4J 23
Skinner St. Chat —5D 8
Skinner St. Gill —3G 9
(in two parts)
Skinners Way. Langl —1K 43
Skua Ct. Roch —1E 6
Skye Clo. Maid —5K 35
Slade Clo. Chat —7F 15
Slatin Rd. Roch —7K 3
Slicketts Hill. Chat —4E 8
Small Profits. Yald —7G 33
Smarts Cotts. Bear —7H 31
Smeed Clo. Sit —5F 21
Smeed Dean Cen. Sit —5E 20
Smetham Gdns. Roch —6K 3
Smith Rd. Chat —6F 15
Smiths Est. S'lng —7C 24
Smith's Hill. W Far —7K 33
Smith St. Roch —2J 7
Snipe Ct. Roch —1E 6
Snodhurst Av. Chat —4C 14
Snodhurst Ho. Chat —2D 14
Snodland By-Pass. Snod —5B 22
Snowdon Av. Maid —6A 30
Snowdon Clo. Chat —2F 15
Snowdon Pde. Maid —6B 30
Solent Gdns. Chat —1F 15
Solomon Rd. Gill —7F 11
Solomon's Rd. Chat —4D 8
Somerfield Clo. Maid —7G 29
Somerfield La. Maid —6G 29
Somerfield Rd. Maid —7G 29
Somerset Clo. Chat —1G 15
Somerset Clo. Sit —5A 20
Somerset Rd. Maid —4B 36
Somner Wlk. Maid —1E 42
Sorrell Rd. Chat —5C 14
Sortmill Rd. Snod —3D 22
South Av. Gill —6A 10
South Av. Sit —6E 20
S. Aylesford Retail Pk. Ayle —3B 28
South Bank. Sut V —6K 43
Southbourne Gro. Chat —5E 14
S. Bush La. Gill —4H 17
South Ct. Maid —3K 35
South Cres. Cox —2F 41
S. Eastern Rd. Roch —1A 8
Southey Way. Lark —6B 22
Southfields. Roch —5K 7
Southill Rd. Chat —5D 8
South La. Sut V —7K 43
South Pk. Bus. Village. Maid —3K 35
South Pk. Rd. Maid —3A 36
South Rd. Chat —1F 9
(Officers' Rd.)
South Rd. Chat —1E 8
(Wood St.)
S. Side Three Rd. Chat —7F 5
South St. Barm —3B 34
South View. Bear —7H 31
Southwark Rd. Roch —2F 7
South Ways. Sut V —6K 43
Southwell Rd. Roch —2E 6
Southwood. Maid —2C 34
Sovereign Boulevd. Chat —6J 9
Sovereign Ct. Roch —2E 6
Sovereigns, The. Maid —7G 29
Spade La. H'lip —4J 17
Spearhead Rd. Maid —4J 29
Spectrum Bus. Cen. Roch —7C 4
Spectrum Bus. Est. Maid —1E 42
Spectrum W. Maid —3G 29
Speedwell Av. Chat —5C 14
Speedwell Clo. Gill —3J 9
Speedwell Clo. Weav —7D 30
Spekes Rd. Hem —3B 16
Speldhurst Ct. Maid —7G 29
Spencer Clo. Chat —4E 14
Spencer Flats. Chat —1F 15
Spencer Way. Maid —5D 36
Spenlow Dri. Chat —1E 24
Spiers, The. Gill —3C 10
Spillway, The. Maid —2G 35
Spindle Glade. Maid —6B 30
Spindlewood Clo. Chat —6F 15
Spinnaker Ct. Roch —7A 8
Spinney, The. Maid —2A 36
Spires, The. Maid —7G 29
Spires, The. Roch —3F 7
Spitfire Clo. Chat —3F 15
Spitfire Rd. W Mal —1A 32
Sportsfield. Maid —6A 30
Sportsmans Cotts. King H —6C 26
Spot Farm Cotts. Maid —5J 37
Spot La. Down —2E 36
(in three parts)
Sprig, The. Bear —7F 31
Spring Cotts. Lin —7G 41
Springett Clo. Eccl —4H 23
Springett Way. Cox —1G 41
Springfield Av. Maid —4J 29
Springfield Rd. Gill —2J 9
Springfield Rd. Lark —7B 22
Springfield Rd. Sit —4B 20
Springfield Ter. Chat —4D 8
Springvale. Gill —3C 16
Spring Vale. Maid —7H 29
Springwood Clo. Maid —1C 34
Springwood Rd. Barm —1D 34
Sprotshill Clo. Sit —3C 20
Spruce Clo. Lark —1H 27
Spurgeon's Cotts. Langl —3H 41
Spurway. Bear —7F 31
Sqaure Hill. Maid —7A 30
Square Hill Rd. Maid —1A 36
Square, The. Hunt —6A 40
Squires Clo. Roch —1D 6
Stable Clo. Chat —4G 15
Stable Cotts. Maid —5F 35
Staceys St. Maid —6J 29
Staffa Rd. Maid —5K 35
Stafford St. Gill —3F 9
Stag Rd. Chat —4G 15
Stagshaw Clo. Maid —2K 35
Stake La. Hall —3C 12
Stalham Ct. Hem —5B 16
Stalin Av. Chat —1F 15
Stampers, The. Maid —2G 35
Standen Clo. Gill —5E 16
Stanford Dri. Maid —1F 35
Stanford Way. Cux —6E 6
Stanhope Av. Sit —6D 20
Stanhope Clo. Maid —4H 29
Stanhope Rd. Roch —1J 7
Stanley Rd. Chat —3G 15
Stanley Rd. Gill —2G 9
Stansted Clo. Maid —4F 29
Staple Clo. Sit —4C 20
Staplehurst Rd. Gill —5B 10
Staplehurst Rd. Sit —5A 20
Staplers Ct. Maid —3A 30
Star Hill. Roch —3B 8
Star La. Gill —1K 15
Star Mill Ct. Chat —6H 9
Star Mill La. Chat —6H 9
Starnes Ct. Maid —6K 29
Station App. Hall —4C 12
Station App. Maid —1J 35
Station Hill. E Far —5D 34
Station Hill Cotts. Maid —5E 34
Station Rd. Cux —6E 6
Station Rd. Dit —2K 27
Station Rd. H'shm —6K 39
Station Rd. Maid —6J 29
Station Rd. N'tn —3D 18
Station Rd. Rain —1F 17
Station Rd. Strood —7K 3
Station St. Sit —5C 20
Steadman Clo. High —2E 2
Steele St. Roch —7J 3
Steelfield Ind. Est. Gill —1K 9
Steerforth Clo. Roch —6A 8
Stephens Pl. Maid —3H 35
Step Style. Sit —7F 21
Sterling Av. Maid —6F 29
Sterling Rd. Sit —7B 20
Stevens Clo. Snod —2C 22
Stevenson Clo. Maid —1J 35
Stevenson Way. Lark —6B 22
Stevens Rd. Eccl —4H 23
Stewart Ho. Chatt —1C 4
Stickens La. E Mal —5F 27
Stilebridge La. Lin —7K 41
Stirling Clo. Gill —5E 16
Stirling Clo. Roch —5J 7
Stirling Rd. W Mal —1A 32
Stockbury Dri. Maid —4G 29
Stockett La. Cox & E Far —2F 41
Stockton Clo. Maid —3A 30
Stoke Rd. Hoo —2J 5
Stoke Rd. Bus. Cen. Hoo —2J 5
Stoneacre Clo. Gill —4D 16
Stoneacre Cotts. Maid —5H 37
Stoneacre La. Otham —4G 37
Stone Cotts. E Far —5C 34
Stone Cotts. Langl —1G 43
Stone Cotts. Maid —3C 36
Stonecross Lea. Chat —7G 9
Stonehorse Ct. Roch —4J 3
Stonehorse La. Roch —4J 3
Stoney Hill. Chat —5F 9
Stony La. Roch —4K 13
Stopford Rd. Gill —4G 9
Stour Clo. Roch —1H 7
Stour Ho. Maid —4C 36
Strand App. Rd. Gill —1J 9
Stratford Av. Gill —1D 16
Stratford La. Gill —1F 17